PERSPECTIVES ON CRITICISM

PERSPECTIVES ON CRITICISM

Edited by
MOHIT K. RAY

ATLANTIC PUBLISHERS AND DISTRIBUTORS

Published by
ATLANTIC PUBLISHERS AND DISTRIBUTORS
B-2, Vishal Enclave, Opp. Rajouri Garden, New Delhi-27
Phones : 5413460, 5429987, 5466842

Sales Office
4215/1, Ansari Road, Darya Ganj, New Delhi-02
Phones : 3273880, 3285873, 3280451
Fax : 91-11-3285873
web : www.atlanticbooks.com
e-mail : info@atlanticbooks.com

ISBN 81-269-0097-0

Typeset at
APD Computer Graphics, Delhi

Printed in India at
Mehra Offset Press, Delhi

PREFACE

Philosophical speculations about the origin of poetry and the nature and function of criticism have engaged the attention of poets and critics for over 2500 years in the West, and still have not arrived at any consensus either regarding the mysterious process of creation or the proper function of literary criticism. In recent years, particularly during the second half of the twentieth century, criticism has grown into a heavy industry with too many schools, theories, and assumptions. As we look at the contemporary critical scene we are at once struck by the extreme scepticism with which the very possibility of criticism is confronted. The stability of a work of art is so aggressively questioned that criticism has virtually lost it proper subject giving rise to complete anarchy. The whole movement of deconstruction, starting with Derrida and zealously followed up by Paul de Man, J.H. Miller, Geoffrey Hartmann and Stanley Fish, to name just a few leading exponents is frankly nihilistic. In the arena of open-ended intertextuality we are caught in a tangled skein. Text, we are told, is just an empty container waiting to be filled with meaning. The text may be meaningful, but nothing is meant.

In this period of confusion, standing on the darkling plain as we are, we must focus on the real function of literary criticism, and save literature from being a casualty in the cross-fire of literary theories. Literary criticism is a discourse on literature, and in this sense it includes comparison and analysis, interpretation and evaluation of specific works of literature. In fact, the term criticism is ultimately derived from the Gree *Krino* which means 'to judge,' and *krites* which means 'a judge.' Dryden in the Preface to *The State of Innocence* (1677) said : "By criticism as it was first instituted by Aristotle, was meant a standard of judgement." Pope in 1711 in his *Essay on Criticism* used the term 'criticism' for judgment and evaluation. Incidentally Kant in his *Critique of Judgment* (1790) recognized the subjectivity of aesthetic judgment but allowed for its universality. Taste may be subjective, but aesthetic judgment must differ from taste and must appeal to an ideal totality of judges. Criticism thus is always historical, comparative and universal.

We should never lose sight of the fact that literary criticism must be *literary criticism,* that is, a literary work must be judged by literary criteria. A literary work may have many kinds of values — as a historical document, as a social document, as a biographical event, as a literary sport. But the value of the work has to be judged by literary criteria alone.

The essays included in this volume precisely try to do that. Keeping their focus sharply on the literary text the critics, by comparison and analysis, have tried to evaluate different authors and their works. In their wider gropings they have also embraced the other areas such as the relation between linguistics, literary criticism, scholarship and teaching, etc.

In the very first essay "Scholarship, Criticism and Teaching of Literature," M.P. Sinha has clearly defined the functions of scholarship and criticism and their bearing on the teaching of literature, because a teacher combines in himself a 'holy trinity' : "a scholar, a critic, and a teacher of literature; the lack of any one of which will make him imperfect."

S.P. Singha in his very perceptive and refreshingly original essay "Aestheticism in Poetry : Debt to John Keats" tries to establish that "Keats contributions to aesthetic theory have not been adequately emphasized," and asserts that "apart from Coleridge, Keats was the only critic of the age to present a comprehensive attitude to poetry."

In "Aesthetics and the Literary Theories of Ruskin" Krishna Singh shows how "Ruskin's aesthetic theories are the product and type of the irreconcilable dilemmas in his thoughts" and reaffirms

Rene Wellek's opinion that "Ruskin's significance in literary criticism is not due to any of his scattered opinions or comments, rather...due to his aesthetics."

In "Literary Criticism and Aesthetics" Sushma Sharma examines the relation between literary criticism and aesthetics and re-evaluates the supreme significance of Longinus as a critic in this respect.

Sukriti Ghoshal in his brilliant essay "The Legacy of the Approriator" has shown how Oscar Wilde in his critical theories had anticipated much of modern criticism.

In "The Concept of Imagination" in I.A. Richards' Anjani Kumar makes a fine analysis of Richards's theory of imagination *vis-à-vis* Coleridge's theory of imagination, and shows how Coleridge's organic aestheticism is "restated by Richards in the modern idiom."

Asit Biswas in his well-researched paper "R.S. Crane : A Neo-Aristotelian" has developed his argument brick by brick to establish how "a true Aristotelian he (Crane) starts with an analysis of the (desired) effect on the readers, and retrospectively identifies the factors that contribute to his effect."

In another equally insightful essay "R.S. Crane and the Theory of Structural Analysis" Asit Biswas suggests that it would be an act of critical myopia to consider Crane just as a formal critic, and asserts that for a fuller understanding of Crane as a literary critic, he must be seen as a critical pluralist.

In "Literature as Knowledge : Tate's Views" by assiduous application of critical exegesis Samiran Majilya shows how Tate's notion of knowledge enshrines for him the core and essence of literature.

V. Sujatha in "F.W. Bateson's Socio-Hisotrical Criticism : Review of Wordsworth's Poetry" convincingly pleads for a fresh look at Bateson's criticism for a better understanding of Wordsworth's poetry.

In "Winters on Hopkins" Bimalendu Kundu critically analysis Womters's views about the weaknesses of Hopkins as a poet and tries to establish that Winter's judgment on Hopkins is rather biased.

In another essay, "Winters of Yeats" Bimalendu Kundu presents Yeats in a new light when, following Winters, he shows how Yeats's bardic tone was mistaken for greatness and how Yeats's influence on the subsequent generation of poets has been more or less pernicious.

Mallikarjun Patil in "Stylistics : An Overview" traces the genealogical ancestry of stylistics in the classical rhetoricians, points out the differences existing in various modern schools regarding its nature and function, highlights its relevance to the study of literature and finally calls attention to the Indian approaches to style as evidenced in the writings of Bhamaha, Anandavardana, Kuntaka, and others.

A.K. Awasthi in his extremely interesting article "The *Panchakriya* Theory and the Criticism of *Hamlet*" examines *Hamlet* in the light of *Panchakriya* theory or the five eternal principles attributed to Lord Shiva.

K.M. Jan's long essay 'Poetry and Criticism" examines the twin aspects of poetry and provides some models of practical criticism.

M.K. Ray tries to provide a guideline for applying different critical theories to a literary work for pedagogical purposes.

Rama Kundu's intellectually scintillating essay "Filling an Empty Container : A Practical Exercise," made out of the different responses of some teacher-students, marks the height of post-modern playfulness in its multiple interpretations of wide range and variety. Oscar Wilde would have turned in his grave to see what the modern critics have made of his essay "The Critic as an Artist."

I am sure that any student of literature will find the essays quite interesting and useful.

I thank all the contributors for their well-researched papers, and my colleague, Professor Rama Kundu for her unstinted help and support in preparing the volume. My special thanks go to Dr. K.R. Gupta, Managing Director of M/s Atlantic Publishers and Distributors, New Delhi for the confidence evinced in me, and also for seeing the book through the press.

MOHIT K. RAY
Editor

CONTENTS

1

Scholarship, Criticism and Teaching of Literature

—M.P. Sinha

A teacher of English is three-in-one : a scholar, a critic and a teacher of literature; the lack of any one of which will make him imperfect. The task of the scholar is to produce an authentic text and its author's biography, of the critic to analyse, interpret and evaluate according to objective and verifiable principles and of the teacher to present the author and the text before the students for the dissemination and advancement of knowledge and inculcation of the qualities in them to read and appreciate literature and acquire the ability to make distinction between the good and the trash. Unfortunately we teachers of English have neglected the first function producing a critical edition and writing a standard biography and concentrated more on the second one. My aim in this paper is to emphasize and explain the fact that all the three are inseparable and only when we combine these three together we can do justice to our profession.

We read and enjoy literature but care little to the definitiveness of the text. We seldom compare different editions. As a student, I read *Hamlet* and the famous line "O, that this too too solid flesh would melt", and listened to my teacher interpreting it in the most lucid way. The text I had was Cambridge Text, as edited by William Addis Wright. When I began teaching I found to my surprise that the line contained the word "sullied" not "solid". This, too, was a Cambridge edition but the editor was J. Dover Wilson. Certainly, Dover Wilson's amendation is correct because the word "sullied" fits better in the context. But it is also that the people who interpreted the time considering the word "sullied" to be "solid" were beside the point. F.O. Mathiessen's interpretation of Herman Melville's phrase "soiled fish of the sea" in the novel *White Jacket* fell flat when the error in print became known. Mathiessen praised the phrase as characteristic of Melville's imagination, landed the metaphysical conceit and admired its moral and psychological implications. Unfortunately, at least for the critic, the word was "coiled" not "soiled". Dr. F.R. Leavis, too, misinterpreted Henry James's style in *Roderick Hudson* first published in 1874. Dr. Leavis analysed the revised 1917 edition of the novel and praised it for "its sustained maturity of theme and treatment". Professor Gordon Ray has pointed out Dr. Leavis's error and commented thus :

> "This leaves him in the position of having proved at length what nobody would think denying that James's writing at the age of sixtyfour has all the characteristics of maturity" (*TCC* 340).

The great drawback of a critic is that he or she takes one edition, analysis and interprets it without paying the required attention to its authenticity. Scholarship is concerned with the establishment of the text as the author actually write it or intended to write it. By "intention" is not meant what I.A. Richards means or what Winsatt and Beardsley consider to be. The scholar tries to read the author's intention when a word is mis-spelt or indistinct or is not available in the manuscript. His field is bibliography and textual criticism. Bibliography is concerned with the art of book production, history of writing, printing, binding, illustrating and publishing. Modern scholars have extended it to every kind of evidence that has relation to an author and his or her work. *Evidence in Literary Scholarship* edited by René Wellek and Alvaro Rebeiro and published by Clarendon Press, Oxford in 1979 is one of the authoritative collections of essays on bibliography. Professor Fredson Bowers, one of the eminent editors of our time, divides bibliography into three subdivisions : analytical bibliography, descriptive bibliography and textual bibliography. He explains these three :

> "The determination of the physical, external form of a book in terms of the technical analysis of its production is the function of analytical bibliography. The application to external form identifies the discipline of descriptive bibliography. The application to internal form or contents, is the concern of textual bibliography" (26-27).

Textual criticism is concerned with the structure of the text, how its different parts — Acts/Chapters/stanzas and sentences/lines and words — are related and how they form a coherent whole and express the author's intention.

Bibliography and textual criticism establish the authentic text for the reader. If there is a clash between a scholar and a critic we have to rely on the scholar because his or her method is impersonal, objective and systematic and can be empirically verified. Bibliography and textual criticism precede literary history and literary criticism; they form the very foundation on which the edifice of literary criticism is built. Editing, determination of a text's date (chronology), authenticity and attribution and source influence are the main fields of bibliography and textual criticism.

The other important function of the scholar is the production of a literary biography. I.A. Richards and the New Critics considered it harmful for the proper reading of a text and excluded it completely in "close reading". It is agreed that an author's biography may sometimes prejudice the reader but in most cases it helps him or her in understanding some of the obscure allusions, allusions that are personal and private. A literary biography may tell the actual people behind the characters in a novel or play or even a short poem. In fact, no work of art can be completely separated from its creator; it always bears the stamp of his or her personality. The reader, too, after finishing a novel or a poem, wants to know about the author. He asks : who wrote it? What kind of person he or she was? Under what circumstances did he or she write it? Are all the events described are a part of his or her personal experience? Do the characters depicted in the text come from real life?

A standard biography explodes myths about writers. Modern biographers after studying church records and school records have proved that Shakespeare was born in a well-to-do middle class family and the school in which he studied maintained a high standard and that his teacher Mr. Jenkins was an Oxonian graduate who taught him Greek and Latin.

The myth that the Band of Avon fled to London because he was to be prosecuted for poaching, too, has been exploded by scholars. Now we are in a better position to know Shakespeare and make comment on Gray's estimate of the poet in "The Progress of Poesy" and Carlyle's in *Hero and Hero Worship*.

Writing biography is a research activity. The goals of a literary biographer are :

(i) disinterested study of the author's life and ideas;
(ii) situational correlation between the literary work and life of the author;
(iii) distinction between fact and fiction;
(iv) avoidance of unnecessary details to make the biography interesting; and
(v) maintenance of an independent point of view to present the author both in light and shade.

These goals determine the task of the biographer. He, like a historian, collects materials from different sources : the author's biography, his autobiographical statements and reminiscences of his friends and other acquaintances and articles and personal interviews. The sources of the data are :

(i) official records, such as the church, school, college, university, corporation, municipality and land record offices;
(ii) information in the semi-official reports like family genealogy, family diary, land revenue receipts and family member's narration;

(iii) the author's statements in magazines, interviews, diaries are letters;

(iv) references to the author by his or her friends, critics and admirers.

After collecting the materials, the biographer marshals them and writes the biography objectively and critically. Professor Haight's biography of George Eliot is an example of a standard biography.

II

The scholar edits the critical edition or definitive edition of a literary work and writes a standard biography of author. The critic's task is the analysis and evaluation of the text and its author. The problem is how to analyse it and how to interpret it. The multiplicity of critical theories bewilder us. We encounter new criticism, Chicago School of Criticism, British Criticism led by I.A. Richards and F.R. Leavis, Marxist criticism, Psycho-analytical criticism, Myth criticism, Phenomenological criticism and its successor Reader-Response theory, structuralism and post-structuralism, Feminist criticism and Deconstruction. Each school of criticism views a literary work in its own way and then recommends a particular method of analysis. And here is the problem. New criticism is almost ahistorical and rejects an author's biography. The great followers of Richards and Brooks exclude even the title of a poem for its critical analysis. There is no doubt that "close reading" is one of the but methods of reading and analysing a literary text. But why does a poet gives a title to a poem?

The post-structuralist critic Roland Barthes considers the title of great importance. He writes :

> "...the function of the title is to mark the beginning of a text, that is, to constitute the text as a commodity. Every title thus has several simultaneous meanings, including at least these two : (i) what it says linked to the contingency of what follows it; (ii) the announcement itself that a piece of literature...is going to follow; in other words, the

title always has a double function : enunciating and deictic" (*MCT* 176).

The "textual analysis" which is very much like "close reading" is practised by the French post-structuralists and they lay a great importance on the significance of the title of a literary work.

Should we follow "close reading" blindly or adopt "textual analysis"? Or follow the traditional method of paraphrasing and summarising? In my opinion we should adopt an eclectic method but must not ignore the title. It is an injustice to students when we give them a poem without its title for critical analysis.

Then comes the task of interpretation. Which theory should we choose. For Cleanth Brooks irony is the principle of structure and paradox is the language of poetry, for I.A. Richards synaesthesis or synthesis is the prime quality of a literary text, Freud's followers explore the different "complexes" and contents of the unconscious, Myth or Archetypal criticism is interested in the mythic figures and the archetypes of literature, Marxist criticism in the contradictions of society and presentation of realism, and Deconstructionist in pointing out how a literary work can be collapsed. Feminist critics are more interested in discovering the problems of women : political injustice, economic injustice, minority status in the male dominated society and gender-bias.

Each theory of criticism has its own value but has its own limitations too. A critic will analyse and interpret a literary work according to the principles of a particular theory and will claim its superiority over others. Let us take the two basic issues.

First, should a writer be a committed writer or non-committal? Most of the critical theories say that he or she should be an impartial observer. Can a writer, a sensitive human being, a sufferer, remain objective? If he is in a happy position he will never go against the establishment nor will raise a voice against the system. Dryden and Johnson could never go against the crown and like them Tennyson and Browning praised the Victorian ideals. Shelley, on the other hand, did not make a compromise with the system; he remained a revolutionary throughout. In fact the distinction between the committed and the non-committed is erroneous. It is better to make distinction between the pro-establishment and the anti-establishment, between those who favour the existing system and those who want a change. The reality is that every writer has a world outlook and although he or she may not express it overtly, his or her ideology is ever present in his or her work in the non-said form. A great writer speaks for the entire humanity.

The second issue is : what makes a literary work great or valuable? In other words why are *Iliad, Odyssey, Aeneid, Divine Comedy*, some plays of Shakespeare, *Paradise Lost, Faust, The Waste Land* and others like those are great? Why do me read *Middlemarch, Pride and Prejudice, David Copperfield, Brothers Karmazov, War and Peace, Anna Karenina, Mother, Madam Bovary, Jean Christophe* and novels like these again and again? Perhaps, no single critical theory will give a comprehensive answer. One will refer to their philosophy of life, the other their literary qualities, the third their psychology and so on. What should we do? How should we interpret and evaluate them? Let us remember that Rudyard Kipling and Somerset Maugham received the Noble Prize but E.M. Forster did not. But we all know that Forster is a far greater novelist than these two. What makes a literary work valuable and great is its depiction of human values, universality of appeal and arousal of the feelings in the reader what the writer actually felt while writing the text, the true voice of feeling.

The third issue is that of the Indian poetics. Recently, some critics began analysing English literary texts on the principles of the *rasa* theory. This experiment led the teachers of English to study the works of Bharata, Mammata, Anandavardhana and Vishwanath in translation. The question is how far can we apply the Indian poetic theory in the analysis of the European texts? It is true that we are culturally different. We did not want a play to end in tragedy but the Westerners considered tragedy superior to comedy. In other words there is a basic difference between

Bharata Muni and Aristotle. Bhasa, Kalidasa, Bhavabhuti and Shudraka wrote plays which are neither pure tragedy nor pure comedy and they cannot be evaluated in Aristotelian terms. Similarly the plays of Aeschylus, Sophocles, Shakespeare and Webster cannot be analysed after the Indian poetic theory. What we have to do is to evaluate the Western literature from the Indian point of view. We can trace those values in the Western literature, which we cherish most. If Desdemona, Othello, Lear, Cordelia, Macbath, and Lady Macbath fascinate us, the reason is that they are human beings like us. The feelings, sentiments, emotions, desires and weaknesses we have in us they too have. In short, they are us. Similarly, the feelings of Mr. Savage in *The Brave New World* are very much Indian. The stories of Tolstoy contain the kind of truth which we all admire. In short, we should trace those elements in the Western literature which are universal and which are present in the Indian social life. *A Passage to India* and *The Near and the Far* are nearer to us than Arun Joshi's *The Strange Case of Billy Biswas* and *The Last Labyrinth*. Arun Joshi's world is a world of fantasy whereas that of Forster or Meyeres is built on a solid ground, essentially Indian.

III

The teacher of literature is armed like the teacher of language. The language teacher has a good knowledge of linguistics and the different approaches and methods of teaching language. The teacher of literature should be a scholar to evaluate the definitiveness of the text he or she is going to teach, be a critic to analyse and interpret the text objectively and systematically and above all be able to present his or her analysis and interpretation in the classroom. We as teachers are responsible for the dissemination of knowledge to the next generation. It is our pious duty to see that all that we are knowing are given to the younger generation without deviation. The greatest hindrance in communication is the semantic gap. The narrower it is, the better for the listener.

In order that we should not widen the semantic gap, it is our prime duty to present our ideas in simple language. Teaching literature does not mean a show of the profundity of knowledge. We can display our knowledge in research papers and scholarly books, if publishers print them. Our duty in the classroom is to lead the inquisitive learners from the darkness of ignorance to the light to knowledge. Our ideals should be the great religious teachers like Buddha, Mahavira, Christ, Shankaracharya, Mohammad, Dayanand Saraswati to name a few, who explained the complexity of reality in simplest words possible and made the ignorant enlightened.

WORKS CITED

Bowers, F., *Bibliography and Textual Criticism*, Oxford : Clarendon Press, 1964.

Hendy, William J. and Max Westbrook, Eds., *Twentieth Century Criticism : Major Statements*, New Delhi : Light and Life Publishers, 1974. Cited as *TCC*.

Lodge, David, ed., *Modern Criticism and Theory,* London : Longman, 1988. Cited as *MCT*.

2

Aestheticism in Poetry : Debt to John Keats

—S.P. Singha

'AESTHETICISM' broadly means a devotion to beauty and to beauty primarily as found in the arts and in whatever is beautiful around us. It is, therefore, quite logical to assume that aestheticism in this broad sense, has existed throughout civilized history. However, the word 'aestheticism' first assumed a distinctive meaning in the late nineteenth century. It attempted to denote something new — not merely a devotion to beauty, but a new conviction of the importance of beauty as compared with — and even in opposition to other values. Aestheticism came to stand for certain ideas about life and art — ideas which then assumed a distinct form and presented a new and serious challenge to more traditional ideas. In England these ideas became recognisable in the mid-to-late Victorian period — certainly from the eighteen-sixties onwards and in France somewhat earlier. Indeed, in the late nineteenth century there appeared a group of artists who distinguished themselves by the importance they attached to literature and the fine arts and to beauty generally.

The word 'beauty' needs a little elucidation. Many attempts have been made to describe or define beauty since the middle ages. The great mediaeval Christian philosopher, Aquinas, defined beauty commonsensically enough, as that which being seen, pleases. Pleases simply as an object of contemplation either via the senses or within the mind itself. Walter Pater, the foremost exponent of the asethetic view, virtually refuses to define beauty in the 'Preface' to *The Renaissance* (1873) :

> Beauty, like all other qualities presented to human experience, is relative; and the definition of it becomes unmeaning and useless in proportion to its abstractness. To define beauty not in the most abstract but in the most concrete terms possible, to find not its universal formula, but the formula which expresses most adequately this or that special manifestation of it, is the aim of the true student of aesthetics. [Pater 1873 : XXV]

For Pater, therefore, beauty is not a bloodless abstraction, rather it is something to be immediately experienced, to be felt upon the pulses. It is in this sense that the word 'beauty' was adopted by the exponents of aestheticism for whom "art for art's sake" became a useful battlecry. And it is in this sense that the word 'beauty' has to be understood with reference to the aesthetes.

It will be pertinent in this context to speak a few words about the origin of the phrase 'art for art's sake'. The phrase is a translation of the French expression *l'art pour l'art,* an expression that was first used by Victor Cousin in his *Cours de Philosophie...*(Paris, 1836). This source is noted in the Supplement (A-G) of the O.E.D. (1992). But there is no earlier example given of the English equivalent than Swinburne's 1872 review of Victor Hugo's *L' Année Terrible* in this Supplement. However, L.M. Findlay in an article draws our attention to a much earlier use of the phrase in English. He refers to an essay on Lamartine in *The Westminster Review* for January 1837 in which the phrase 'art for art's sake' was used. Referring to Lamartine, the author of the essay writes : "Very fortunately for the young poet, the systematic prefaces, the resuscitation of the poetry of the sixteenth century, the theories of art for art's sake...were still dormant in the heads whence they were afterwards to issue armed, in the costume of barons of the Middle Ages" [Findlay 1973 : 246-48]. It is thus quite apparent that it was in 1837 that the French phrase *l'art pour l'art* was translated into English as 'art for art's sake'.[1]

In order to understand the implications of the phrase we have to examine it in its historical perspective. Towards the middle of the nineteenth century in France and in England (a little later) people got seriously concerned with the value and nature of art and with the relation of art to life. What was the place of art in relation to other values such as morality and material utility? The question was not new but the issues became an unprecedentally sensitive one in mid-nineteenth century. There developed a tendency to seek in literature and the arts and in the appreciation of beauty generally, a complete answer to the individual's need for personal fulfilment, for something to give meaning to his life. Art for Art's Sake was one application of this general tendency, a tendency for which the most comprehensive term is aestheticism. Many critics hold that the theory of art for art's sake arose as a result of a crisis of faith experienced in the late nineteenth century. George Plekhanov in his essay entitled "On Art for Art's Sake" states clearly that "the belief in art for art's sake arises whenever the artist is out of harmony with his social environment" [Craig 1975 : 272].

Late nineteenth century was an extraordinarily varied period when one notices many conflicting schools and tendencies — decadence and counter-decadence, aestheticism and activism, naturalism and symbolism etc.[2] But beneath the diversity there was a major transformation taking place in man's imaginative orientation to the world. The literature of the age gives us convincing clues that behind the surface diversity there was, in fact, a single cultural crisis at work. The diversity of moods and motives may best be viewed as varied responses evoked by a single challenge posed to man's imaginative life. Let us now try to sketch the nature of this challenge. In the early part of the nineteenth century two fundamental axioms prevailed. There was, in the first place, a belief that somewhere within or behind or beyond the world of observable experience, existed an eternal and credible truth. In the second place, it was assumed that man possessed a faculty capable of at least dimly perceiving that truth. Both these axioms were substantially demolished with the advance of science and its implied cosmology — Lyell in geology, Strauss and Renan in the higher criticism of the Bible. Darwin in Biology, Marx in social sciences, Freud in psychology and the rest. As a result, man's age-old faith in God and religion crumbled down. One notices an ominous spread of disbelief during the period that culminates in Nietzsche's assertion : "God hath died". The theme reverberates throughout the age : "Religion is done for — any sort of religion"; we are "dying slowly and surely of Unbelief — and there can be no deadlier disease" [Nietzsche 1892 : Part IV]. With the collapse of the old religious faith came an impulsive search for new ones. Thus in 1875 the Theosophical Society was founded, in 1878 the Salvation Army was established, in 1882 was founded the Society for Psychical Research, in 1888 was founded the Ethical Culture Society. The list could go on to include Esoteric Buddhist Society, Hermetic Society and the rest.[3]

Thus, as a result of the challenge man was robbed of any unassailable framework of values. The old certainties became uncertain; man was called on to live with a world of flux and chance within which he had to grope his way in uncertainty. The human Heart, the Mind and the Imagination responded differently to this central challenge. Responses of the heart mean those responses which are directly and primarily emotional. Much of the most prevalent emotional response was the mood of pessimism. Almost everyone felt the onslaught of despair directly in their own lives, felt themselves members of a —

> "...miserable race! Too weak to bear,
> Too sad for mirth, too sceptical for prayer!"
>
> [Davidson 1895 : 87]

Thus pessimism became the prevalent mood but along with this there was also the growth of activism. Paradoxically, the two moods are related to a degree. But our concern here is not with the responses of the heart, so let us leave the matter without going into the details. Responses of the mind mean those responses which are primarily intellectual in nature. By far the most prevalent intellectual response of the age, indeed the predominant intellectual attitude was that of scepticism — a desire to circumvent, or escape from the confines of scientific reasoning. Closely allied with this distrust of scientific thought was the interest in the esoteric, occult and oriental mysticism. As this is also not our concern here, we drop the issue without getting into the details.

The overwhelming response of the imagination was the longing for aesthetic pleasure as a separate, refined, world-defying element in man's existence. Wearing wide Byronic collar and breeched in velvet, Oscar Wilde declared to his audience in New York (1882) : "There is but one time, the artistic moment, but one law, the law of form; but one land, the land of beauty"[4] [Wilde 1882 : 13]. Much of the rage for art can be explained by the fact that art came to be regarded as offering a shelter and solace to the disillusioned heart in the face of the growing preoccupation with material progress and concerns. "To live through a single day with an overpowering consciousness of our real position", thought Arthur Symons, "would drive any man out of his senses" [Symons 1899 : 1721]. But to this plight art was a solace and "before all things an escape" [Symons 1899 : 173]. This idea impelled the writers and artists during this period to glorify art, insisting sometimes even flamboyantly on its independence from all earthly things. Thus to the aesthetes art was required to be as free as possible from all ulterior motives — social, ethical or ideological. Sometimes they even demanded that art needed to be free from any attributable meaning. One manifestation of the demand becomes evident in the virtually universal acceptance of music as the form towards which all arts must 'constantly aspire' [Pater 1873 : 111]. Again, the various attempts to make poetry approximate to the plastic arts were undertaken deliberately during this period to emphasize the idea of autonomy of art, to make poetry independent of ideas, debates, anecdotes and exteriorities of all kinds.[5]

The quest for salvation through art ultimately resulted in the transformation of art into a substitute religion. This is the central mythology of the Aesthetic Movement — a proclamation of the

Religion of Art. The adoption of art as a substitute of religion was an ironic inversion of spiritual loyalties on the part of many who in the late nineteenth century either lost their Christian faith or had suffered from an unsettling doubt. The quest for this new religion which may also be termed as an alternative value-system is dramatically told by W. B. Yeats who, in his *Autobiographies* reveals that Huxley and Tyndall had deprived him of the "simple minded religion" of his childhood. The alternative was not atheism but art, the means by which to regenerate his spiritual life : "I had made a new religion, almost an infallible church of poetic tradition.... I had even created a dogma" [Yeats 1965 : 77]. Even Arnold in "The Study of Poetry" (1880) had written that "more and more mankind will discover that we have to turn to poetry to interpret life for us, to console us, to sustain us" [Arnold 1903 : 2]. By the end of the century Arthur Symons wrote that literature "in speaking to us so intimately, so solemnly as only religion had hitherto spoken to us...became itself a kind of religion, with all the duties and responsibilities of the sacred ritual" [Symons 1899 : 172]. The point that I wish to make is that an attempt was made during the late nineteenth century to substitute art as an alternative to religion. Karl Beckson calls this the "Central Mythology of the Aesthetic Movement : The Religion of Art and Beauty" [Beckson 1974 : 233-45]. Like all religions 'the Religion of Art' had its sacred texts. In a sonnet on Gautier's *Mademoiselle de Maupin*, famed for its Preface proclaiming *l'art pour l'art*. Swinburne called the novel "the golden book of spirit and sense/The Writ of holy beauty" [Lang 1968 : 381]. Oscar Wilde borrowed the line from Swinburne to characterise Pater's *The Renaissance* (1873).[6] In fact, *The Renaissance* served upon its appearance as the manifesto of the Aesthetic Movement. Pater's responses to the crisis of faith are recorded in *The Renaissance*. Pater seems to suggest that in the face of the ephemeral and transitory quality of the world of phenomena our only hope lies in endowing the fleeting moments of life with the highest quality of enrichment. For Pater art is capable of doing this. He, therefore, recommends the pursuit of art as a means of enriching our moments : "Of such wisdom, the poetic passion, the desire of beauty, the love of art for its own sake, has most. For art comes to you proposing frankly to give nothing but the highest quality to your moments as they pass, and simply for those moments' sake" [Pater 1873 : 198-99].

As a view of art aestheticism represents a drastic attempt to separate art from life. Most people would accept that art is different from life; but the aesthetic standpoint emphasises that difference to the point of saying that art has no reference to life, therefore no social, moral/ethical concern. A work of art is not to be valued for anything that could influence our conduct or even our general attitude to life; it is to be valued solely for the immediate aesthetic pleasure it affords. This is a development having many implications. One of them is that it led artists to attach a high value to form, to regard a work of art as being dependent on form rather than on content. The eighteenth century aesthetics regarded language as the dress of thought — the implication is that thought is more important than language. The extreme aesthetic position reverses the idea and represents the dress as the really important thing. The thought is merely the shopwindow model on which the dress is displayed. Underlying such views is the assumption that literature ought to free itself from all that is not literature. Literature is viewed as an impure art because it is dependent, unlike music and the plastic arts, on ideas. This can be overcome by making literature emulate the plastic arts. Pater and Swinburne's keen interest in painting encouraged them to regard a work of literature as an art-object, an artefact. This led to what George Moore considered as "pure poetry"[7] — poetry which conveys no more comment on life than a flower-vase. Relevant developments in the field of literature, more precisely poetry, may be pointed out thus — (a) a movement away from contemporary life into realms of exotic fantasy, (b) the depiction, especially in poetry, of states of mind that were formerly considered either suspect or not fit for public consumption, (c) a high valuation of sensuous, specially visual imagery, (d) a certain vagueness of subject-matter. The last effect was achieved by subordinating the precise use of language to the quasi-musical evocation of mood.

The literary implications of aestheticism were brought out most clearly in connection with poetry. Aestheticism in England, in spite of the important continental influence on it, may be viewed as a natural development from English romantic literature and romantic ideas about the creative imagination. According to Raymond Williams, "what was called, from Pater in the late 'sixties, the new doctrine of 'art for art's sake' was really little more than a restatement of an attitude which properly belongs to the first generation of the Romantics" [Williams 1958 : 166]. Indeed, seeds of aesthetic indifference to moral/ethical issues were latent in romanticism itself, especially in the works of John Keats. Wilde in 1887 called him the "Priest of Beauty slain before his time" and at his grave composed a poem in which he compares Keats to Guido's portrait of St. Sebastian gazing "towards the Eternal Beauty of the opening heavens" :

> "The youngest of the martyr here is lain,
> Fair as Sebastian and as foully slain."
>
> [Ellmann 1970 : 3-5]

Indeed Keats's contributions to aesthetic theory have not been adequately emphasised. Apart from Coleridge, Keats was the only critic of the age to present a comprehensive attitude to poetry.

The relation between the subjective and the objective, the world of phenomena and the world of mind; the antithesis between the world of senses and the world of ideas — these two problems greatly occupied the romantic theorists. They tried to solve the problem by stressing the sublime and vital function of man's imagination. To Coleridge imagination is the shaping spirit reconciling all contraries while Wordsworth talks of giving to ordinary objects a certain colouring of imagination. The romantic emphasis on imagination discredited any rigid rule of neo-classicism and narrow realism and led to the acceptance of the world of poetry as different from — if related to — the world of reality. Wordsworth, of course, did not recognise the possibility of any separation between meaning and ideas in a poem and the imaginative power with which it makes its impact upon the reader. Coleridge also believed that poetic truth could be made synonymous with philosophical truth and hoped that Wordsworth's *The Prelude* would demonstrate this. But the reality sadly disappointed him and one notices a shift in Coleridge's stand in "On the Principles of Genial Criticism". One needs to recognise the full relevance of his detachment of "beauty for its own sake" from the tyranny of "connection or association with some other thing" [Shawcross 1907 : 236]. And with Coleridge's capitulation it became natural for the later Romantic poets to try for this separation. Keats was always haunted by this division between poetry and philosophy. "What the imagination seizes as Beauty must be Truth" [Letters 1987 : 37] — seems only to be his uneasy attempt to assert a unity between the two. Indeed, Keats's seemingly casual remarks in his letters contain seeds of ethical indifference and his sense of uneasiness because of the wide gap between empirical truth and imaginative truth.

There is a growing tendency in modern criticism to argue that Keats's letters are finer than his poetry because the volatility and mobility of Keats's mind and temperament are recorded in, the letters with a directness impossible in the poems. According to John Barnard, "It is quite possible to read the letters in their own right as the autobiography of Keats's imaginative quest" [Barnard 1987 : 144]. With the exception of the verse-epistles, the letters were written simply as letters yet some of the most remarkable critical observations appear unexpectedly as he passes from one trifle to another in the course of his private correspondence. His observations on the nature of poetry, imagination and beauty represent the finest quality of criticism and in the words of Eliot "keep pretty close intuition" [Eliot 1933 : 102]. Here he discusses, as Douglas Bush noted, four important questions : Has the artist any right to exist in a world full of chaos and suffering? If we allow him to exist, should his imagination be self-centred, or should it be dramatic and impersonal? Should the poet arrive at truth by sensuous intuition or by deliberate thought and reason? These are the inner conflicts he shared with his correspondents and to which he attempted answers. In doing so, he gave an impetus to the ideals of aestheticism.

Keats held that poetry is not meant to communicate or express a philosophy or a religious doctrine or any theory about social or political outlook. Poetry has to reveal beauty. This beauty is an abiding verity uncontaminated by conventions and customs. Rejecting the didactic element in poetry he writes in a letter to Reynolds (3 Feb. 1818), "We hate poetry that has a palpable design upon us...Poetry should be great and unobtrusive, a thing which enters one's soul" [Letters 1987 : 61]. In a letter to John Taylor (27 Feb. 1818) while appreciating the minor alterations made by Taylor to *Endymion*, Keats expresses some of his axioms about poetry. He states quite clearly that "if Poetry comes not as naturally as the leaves to a tree it had better not come at all" [Letters 1987 : 70]. Elsewhere he seems to accept, much more characteristically, poetry as being a purely natural activity, like eating or breathing as opposed to the superior, non-natural field of philosophy or morals. Any "graceful instinctive attitude" constitutes poetry's material and inspiration; and Keats using the same significant word, remarks a few sentences earlier in the letter to George and Georgiana Keats (March 19, 1819), "I myself am pursuing the same instinctive course as the veriest human animal you can think of" [Letters 1987 : 230]. He explains that "though a quarrel in the streets is a thing to be hated, the energies displayed in it are fine"; and that these instinctive energies are "the very thing in which consists poetry; and so it is not so fine a thing as philosophy — for the same reason that the eagle is not so fine a thing as truth" [Letters 1987 : 230]. It becomes quite clear that Keats accepted the idea of diminution in the status of poetry and the fact that it was imprisoned in the domain of the 'natural'. We must remember, too, that though he had most likely not heard them formulated in any philosophical sense, Kantian notions were much in the air at the time through influence of Coleridge; and Kant had stressed that there is no goodness in Nature as such, that all moral values must be non-natural — a view with which many of the aesthetes of the late nineteenth century would have fully agreed. Again, if we analyse the statement of Keats it becomes quite apparent that he makes a distinction between ethics and aesthetics; and he is convinced that the yardstick for the one does not apply to the other. "A quarrel in the street" is to be hated from the ethical point of view but when viewed purely from the aesthetic standpoint "the energies displayed in it are fine".

This idea of a self-oriented aestheticism is latent in the famous Keatsian concept of 'Negative Capability'. The phrase 'Negative Capability' reflects a rare insight into creative psychology although it does not have the precision and rigour of a philosophical concept. But the way it has stimulated and baffled commentators shows that the phrase is rich enough to defy any restrictive use and meaning. It has been pointed out by many that Keats was greatly indebted to William Hazlitt in conceiving the idea. Hazlitt in his lecture "On Shakespeare and Milton" (*Lectures on the English Poets*) spoke of Shakespeare's protean capacity for transforming himself at will into any character he chose. Keats who attended Hazlitt's lectures was greatly influenced by the idea but to overstress that and treat Keats's idea as an appendage to Hazlitt's, as René Wellek does (*A History of Modern Criticism, Vol. II, The Romantic Age*), is to misrepresent Keats. In December 1817 Keats offers his formulation of 'negative capability' in his letter to George and Tom : "...several things dovetailed in my mind & at once it struck me, what quality went to form a Man of Achievement, especially in literature and which Shakespeare possessed so enormously — I mean Negative Capability, that is when a man is capable of being in uncertainties, mysteries, doubts, without any irritable reaching after fact and reason —" [Letters 1987 : 43]. Keats suggests that our life is full of uncertainties and no single formula or system can explain everything. Reason or

Philosophy seeks to impose a pattern on reality which the speculative mind rejects as arbitrary. Scepticism — resulting in pluralism and ambiguity — is here defended as a positive faith. The antithesis of the philosopher and the speculative mind is elaborated by an analogy of the bee and the flower : "...let us not therefore go hurrying about and collecting honeybee like, buzzing here and there impatiently from a knowledge of what is to be arrived at : but let us open over leaves like a flower and be passive and receptive [Letters 1987 : 66].

If Keats here advocates a non-intellective mode of perception, his observations to Woodhouse (27 Oct. 1818) emphasise the non-moral attitude of the ideal poetical character. The ideal poetical character as distinguished from the egotistical sublime, "has no self — it is everything and nothing — It has no character it enjoys light and shade; it lives in gusto, be it foul or fair, high or low, rich or poor, mean or elevated — It has as much delight in conceiving an Iago as an Imogen. What shocks the virtuous philosopher, delights the camelion poet" [Letters 1987 : 157]. Keats suggests here that the poetical character has no specific identity of its own, for it can be at home in any situation. It does not hate evil nor does it side with the good. It is capable of identifying itself with an Iago as much as it does with a Miranda. It is more than obvious that the self-projection or imaginative identification precluded any moral/ethical or conceptual bias. The poet in his eagerness to represent sensuous beauty may become indifferent to all social, moral or ideological concerns. This separation of ethics from aesthetics contributed towards the growth of aestheticism in the late nineteenth century. It will be interesting to note that Oscar Wilde used the words of Keats in defending his novel, *The Picture of Dorian Gray* (1890) against an unjust criticism of a reviewer in the *Scots Observer*. In a letter to the editor of the Journal, the *Scots Observer* (9 July, 1890) Wilde writes, "Of one who is the greatest figure in the world's literature since Greek days, Keats remarked that he had as much pleasure in conceiving the evil as he had in conceiving the good. Let your reviewer, sir, consider the bearings of Keats's fine criticism, for it is under these conditions that every artist works.... Your reviewer suggests that I do not make it sufficiently clear whether I prefer virtue to wickedness or wickedness to virtue. An artist, sir, has no ethical sympathies at all. Virtue and wickedness are to him simply what the colours on his palette are to the painter...Iago may be morally horrible, and Imogen stainlessly pure. Shakespeare, Keats said, had as much delight in creating the one as he had in creating the other" [Ellmann 1973 : 247-48]. I quote rather a long excerpt from Wilde's letter only to emphasise the point that Wilde understood the full implication of Keats's statement which advocates a separation between ethics and aesthetics and employed it in defence of his controversial novel, *The Picture of Dorian Gray* (1890).

Again, Keats's letter to Shelley written on 16 August 1820, bears testimony to Keats's aesthetic sympathies and associates him with the ideals of aestheticism from another perspective. The letter records Keats's reactions on receiving a copy of Shelley's *Cenci* : "I received a copy of the *Cenci*, as from yourself from Hunt. There is only one part of it I am judge of; the Poetry and dramatic effect, which by many spirits now-a-days is considered the mammon...an artist must serve Mammon — he must have 'self-concentration', selfishness perhaps..." [Letters 1987 : 389-90]. It goes without saying that Keats hardly shared Shelley's political and social passions. He did not see the poet as the trumpet that sings to battle. or the unacknowledged legislators of mankind. For Keats, an artist must serve Mammon — that is, his own art rather than any social/political cause. And this devotion to his work is to an artist an all-absorbing passion that makes him indifferent to and oblivious of all other considerations. This requires a 'self-concentration' which might for all practical purposes, make the artist appear to the world as selfish. By laying such an emphasis on the devotion to art (in the sense of conscious artistry) Keats also anticipates the conscious glorification of craftsmanship which marked the aesthetes. Indeed the late nineteenth century aesthetes considered efforts towards style as a sacred duty. It is this artistic discipline, the sense of martyrdom to style that constitutes one of the chief legacies of the aesthetic movement. Even T.S. Eliot had to admit that "the theory of art for art's sake is still valid in so far as it can be taken as an exhortation to the artist to stick to his job" [Eliot 1986 : 442]. It is in the context of Keats's insistence on the art of poetry that one has to understand Keats's exhortation to Shelley : "You, I am sure, will forgive me for sincerely remarking that you might curb your magnanimity and be more of an artist, and 'load every rift' of your subject with ore" [Letters 1987 : 390]. It was Keats's deep conviction that formal discipline alone can give poetry a firm structure and significance. Keats is above everything else a conscious artist who is anxious to load every rift of his verse with its special kind of excellence.

In this insistence on the art of poetry to the exclusion of all practical purposes, Keats anticipates the artist who wished to carve a separate kingdom for the arts and this letter, Graham Hough believes, "marks the beginning in England of the doctrine that was later to develop into Art for Art's sake" [Hough 1953 : 157]. However, it is only the beginning; and the development belongs to an altogether different and later story. Keats is never quite happy in the belief and never works out its implications to his own satisfaction. What he says to Shelley in this letter can be countered by what he says elsewhere — that the magnanimity of sharing the distresses of humanity is essential to the poet's growth. He probably grew aware of the sterility of this selfish aesthetic pursuit of beauty as is evident in his last poetic testament, "The Fall of Hyperion". The pilgrim-poet in "The Fall" seeks to reach the summit of poetic knowledge but before he can continue his quest, he is questioned and told that —

> None can usurp this height,...
> But those to whom the miseries of the world
> Are misery, and will nor let them rest.
> All else who find a haven in the world,
> Where they may thoughtless sleep away their days,
> Rot on the pavement where thou rotted'st half.
>
> [Allott 1970 : 667]

Barbara Charlesworth in her *Dark Passages : Decadent Consciousness in Victorian Literature* (Univ. of Wisconsin Press, 1965) comes to the conclusion that the poets of the aesthetic movement perished on the pavement because in the spacious haven of their own imaginations they thoughtlessly slept away their days. But in Keats the poetic self is not altogether isolated from its surroundings and "the gates of imaginations" to use Professor Kermode's words, "seemed to be open to every human being" [Kermode 1957 : 110]. Even an early poem like *Endymion* which had been so adversely criticised by contemporary reviewers illustrates the idea that love of beauty, like all other passions, cannot exist fruitfully in isolation, that it can only fulfil itself through participations in the actual conditions of life. The point becomes clear when one compares *Endymion* with Shelley's *Alastor* both of which exploit an identical theme. While *Alastor* emphasise a blank dichotomy between the world of experience and the world of imagination *Endymion* rejects this antinomy through the sudden transformation of the Indian maid into Cynthia.

The relation of art, his own kind of art, to human life as a whole was a question that perplexed Keats throughout his life. He had clear and unmistakable aesthetic predilections but these are constantly kept in check by human concerns. Or, it might also be said that he could never outgrow the influences of his age. He lived, as we know, in an age when a smack of the philanthropist, the friend of humanity was expected of liberal and enthusiastic youth; and he began his career in a circle of liberal enthusiasts. In this connection, it may be interesting to point out that much contemporary criticism pays an extensive attention to the political subtext of Keats's writings. One may refer to the special number of *Studies in Romanticism* on "Keats and Politics" Vol. XXV, No. 2 (Summer, 1986) and Daniel P. Watkins's book *Keats's Poetry and the Politics of Imagination* (Cranbury, 1989). Such developments are to be viewed in the context of the growing interest in postcolonical theory which for the first time marginalises the formalist trends which had a long tradition in the present century from Russian Formalism to Deconstruction. But in spite of his association with the liberal enthusiasts of his age, Keats could never really worry himself about many of the things that worried his friends. He felt obscurely of a great liberal of the past that he was not quite a "friend to humanity" and we find Keats wondering "Whether Milton's apparently less anxiety for Humanity proceeds from his farther or no than Wordsworth" [Letters 1987 : 93]. Indeed it may safely be affirmed that all through the much-discussed changes and developments in his poetry, the aesthetic sympathies remained active.

NOTES

1. In this connection one may also refer to Singer's essay entitled "The Aesthetics of Art for Art's Sake" published in the *Journal of Aesthetics and Art Criticism*, Vol. XXII, 1954, 343-59. R.V. Johnson's *Aestheticism* (Methuen, 1969) is also very useful.
2. For a fuller account of this phenomenon see the essays in Richard Ellmann ed. *Edwardians and Late Victorians*, Columbia University Press, 1960. The problem has also been dealt with in Ruth Z. Temple's essay "Truth in Labelling : Pre-Raphaelitism, Aestheticism, Decadence, Fin De Siecle"; *English Literature in Transition*, Vol. XVII, No. IV, 1974.
3. A comprehensive discussion of the issue is available in John Lester's *Journey Through Despair, 1880-1914 : Transformation in British Literary Culture* (New Jersey : Princeton University Press, 1968).
4. Oscar Wilde's essay "The English Renaissance of Art" was first given as a lecture in New York during his American tour sponsored by the D'oyly Carte Opera Company. The essay which is regarded as a full-length manifesto of aestheticism is reprinted in Derek Stanford ed. *Writing of the 'Nineties* (Everyman's Library, London, 1971). The essay clearly shows Wilde's profound respect for Keats.
5. One of the major objectives of the aesthetes in the late nineteenth century was to achieve an assimilation of the impulses of the different arts. Gautier's *Emaux et Cameés* (1852), poems of which are little pictures, on cameo or enamel, provided the model. The eccentric American painter James McNeill Whistler's Ten O'Clock Lecture gave the theoretical justification for it. For a discussion on this issue see Graham Hough's *The Last Romantics* (1947; Methuen, 1961).
6. Cited in Richard Ellmann ed. *The Artist As Critic : Critical Writings of Oscar Wilde* (W.H. Allen, London, 1970), p. 230.

7. The final development of nineteenth century views of 'pure poetry' is perhaps represented by the Irish writer George Moore (1852-1933) who in his later years published an anthology with an introduction — *Pure Poetry* (1924) — designed to expound and illustrate his idea of what was and was not validly poetic.

WORKS CITED

Allot, Miriam, ed., *The Complete Poems of John Keats*, London : Longman, 1970.

Arnold, Matthew, *Essays in Criticism,* 2nd Series, London : Macmillan, 1903.

Barnard, John, *John Keats,* London : Cambridge UP, 1987.

Beckson, Karl, "A Mythology of Aestheticism," *English Literature in Transition*, Vol. XVII, No. IV.

Coleridge, S.T. *Biographia Literaria*, ed. Shawcross, London : 1907, ii.

Craig, David, ed., *Marxists on Literature : An Anthology*, London : Pangwin., 1975.

Davidson, John, "Mr. Grosse's Poems", *Illustrated London News,* Jan. 19, 1895.

Eliot, T.S., *The Use of Poetry and the Use of Criticism*, London : Faber and Faber, 1964. First published in 1937.

——, *Selected Essays*, London, Faber and Faber, 1966.

Ellmann, Richard, ed., *The Artist As Critic : Critical Writings of Oscar Wilde*, London : W.H. Allen, 1970.

Findlay, L.M., "The Introduction of the Phrase 'Art for Art's Sake' in English", *Notes and Queries,* Vol. XX, No. VII, 1973.

Gittings, Robert, ed., *Letters of John Keats*, (London : O.U.P., 1987).

Hough, Graham, *The Romantic Poets*, 1953; Indian Reprint, 1980.

Kermode, Frank, *Romantic Image*, London : Routedge, 1957.

Lang, Cecil Y., ed., *The Pre-Raphaelites and Their Circles*, New York : Houghton, Mifflin, 1968.

Nietzsche, Friedrich, *Thus Spake Zarathustra,* trans. Alexander Tille, London : 1892 : 1896.

Pater, Walter, *The Renaissance*. 1873, New York, The Modern Library, n.d.

Stanford, Derek, ed., *Writing of the 'Nineties,* London : Everyman's Library, Dent, 1971.

Symons, Arthur, *The Symbolist Movement in Literature*. N.Y. : 1899; E.P. Dutton & Co., 1919.

Williams, Raymond, *Culture and Society*. 1987; London : Hogarth Press, 1993.

Yeats, W.B., *Autobiographies,* N.Y. : Collier Books, 1965.

3

Aesthetics and the Literary Theories of Ruskin

—*Krishna Singh*

RUSKIN'S theory of aesthetics provides him a permanent place in the realm of literature. It has been propounded in the first three volumes of *Modern Painters* (1843, 1846, 1856) and later in his social writings in which art assumes a central place. His idiosyncracies and robust social utterances cannot obscure his theory of art, which is far from incoherent or, even old fashioned; but an impressive restatement of romantic organism. Ruskin's aesthetics apply to literature for he always refused to draw a line between the painter and the poet, he uses the word *poetry* often in the wide Platonic sense, and he moves indiscriminately from painting or sculpture to poetry and back again. The unity of arts is not merely assumed; it follows from a theory that makes creation an internal act of intuition and imagination. The central doctrine of organism is held by Ruskin consistently throughout his life, even though there were shifts of emphasis. According to Hugh Walker in the aesthetics theory, "nothing is more remarkable than the cotnrolling influence of *the spirit/of medievalism*" (712). It is obviously drawn largely from Wordsworth and Coleridge and from Carlyle whom Ruskin acknowledges as his master. His work on Beautiful and Imagination holds a unique place. Ball tells us that Ruskin was from the early time, determined to investigate the *faculty or source from which the pleasure given by any poem or passage was derived* (14).

Ruskin's theory of beautiful embodies the concern, methods and dilemma which characterise all his writings. His aesthetic theories provide what Ruskin would have called a type, an emblem, of all his thought. In the first place, both the origin and development of these aesthetic formulations are characteristic of his works whether on art or political economy; for he shaped his theories of beauty — like his theories of economics — polemically. Which is to say, he formed them in conscious opposition to ideas he wished to confute and paid careful attention to the way his theories served such a purpose. Secondly they embody that characteristically Victorian eclecticism which appeared throughout his thought. His conception of Typical and Vital Beauty draws upon Aristotle, Plato, Hooker, Bacon, Pope, Dr. Johnson, Wordsworth, Reynolds and many others, they combine notions derived from neoclassical poetry and criticism. Evengelical Anglican conceptions of scripture, and the late 18th century Scottish moral philosophers. Such an assemblage of often contradictory sources well provide an emblem for the vigour, style and dilemma which mark off the Victorian ideas from those of the past. Like Tennyson and Arnold who return to the ancient and medieval legends for materials with which to make a poetry relevant to contemporary life. Ruskin consciously attempts to enrich the present with the forms and inspiration of earlier times. This use of eclectically gathered writings is most evident in his theories of the beautiful, for in setting forth these theories. According to Landow Ruskin was concerned to demonstrate *the orderly nature of beauty by relating it to a vision of universal order* (15).

All Ruskin's aesthetic theory is permeated with religious spirit. He finds all over nature certain external qualities which are *typical of divine attributes, and it is these qualities which constitute beauty. This beauty is absolutely the same whether found in man, beast or stone, and exists everywhere. These typical qualities which Ruskin finds in nature are six : Infinity — typical of Divine Incomprehensibility, Unity — typical of Divine Comprehensiveness, Symmetry — typical of Divine Justice,*

Purity — typical of Divine Energy and Moderation — typical of Divine Government by law (Works Vol. 3 : 111). This class of beauty Ruskin calls *Typical Beauty* which is the stamp of God's image on whatever He has created.

The traditional notions of beauty which Ruskin incorporates into his own aesthetics appear under these six headings, and their inclusion is apt for Typical Beauty is an aspect of Universal order and those traditional aesthetic theories which emphasise the orderliness of beauty, or its dependence upon order, here find a ready place.

Order in nature and art was an 18th century concept which Ruskin adopted. Order in nature and its recreation or representation in art is related to the idea that perceptions of order is itself pleasing, and that order produces all or part of the phenomenon of beauty. Ruskin believes that order itself is a primary cause of the beautiful or better, that order is itself beautiful. This belief lies at the centre of Ruskin's theory of Typical Beauty. In outlining his theory Ruskin shows that all forms of Typical Beauty please because these forms symbolize divine order in material things. Similarly, when he explains the individual forms of this kind of beauty he shows that they relate to a vision of universal, pleasing order.

In setting forth the theory of unity amid variety Ruskin emphasises the first term *unity* and this stress on the element of order is in agreement to the writings of his old friend and teacher, the artist J.D. Harding; *variety is essential to beauty, and is so inseparable from it, that there can be no beauty where there is no variety* (39). But Ruskin goes ahead, believes that variety is not itself beautiful. It is therefore only *harmonious and chordal variety which is necessary to secure and extend unity...which is rightly agreeable; and so I name not variety as essential to beauty, because it is only so in a secondary and casual sense* (Works Vol. 4 : 96-97). The final emphasis, for Ruskin, must be upon the divine element of unity, one of the most important laws of the universe. Unity is perfected by variety : *Essential unity* which binds *things separately imperfect into a perfect* (Work Vol. 4 : 95) *and hence out of the necessity of unity, arises that of variety* (Works 4 : 95-96). Thus unity, the order which is a symbol and manifestation of external order, is the major term in Ruskin aesthetic formula.

After he has explained the theory of unity amid variety, Ruskin proceeds to his second aesthetic formulation of order, the theory that proportion is beauty. He derives proportion, the ordered relation of qualities, from a form of unity different from that mentioned in relation to the beauty of unity and variety. The beauty of unity and variety arises when *harmonious and chordal variety* creates the unity of membership, *that unity of things separately imperfect into a perfect whole* (Works 4 : 95). Proportion on the other hand, creates a unity of sequence, a unity which is the ordering principle in changing, developing things. Ruskin explains how this kind of Typical Beauty symbolises a principle of the physical and moral world. Thus the unity of sequence is *that of things that form links in chains, and steps in accents, and stages in journeys; and this, in matter, in the unity of communicable forces is their continuance from one thing to another; and it is the passing upwards and downwards of beneficent effects among all things, the melody of sounds, the continuity of lines and the orderly succession of motions and times and in spiritual creatures it is their own constant building up, by true knowledge and continuous reasoning, to higher perfection; and the singleness and straightforwardness of their tendencies to more complete communion with God* (Works 4 : 94-95).

The second form of proportion, that with which Ruskin is primarily concern is apparent proportion, which *takes place between quantities for the sake of connection only, without any ultimate object or casual necessity* (Works 4 : 102). This apparent proportion, a law of nature, *which is itself seemingly; the end of operation to many of forces of nature, is therefore at root of all over delight in any beautiful form whatsoever* (Works 4 : 107-108).

This belief in the importance and beauty of order also informs Ruskin's brief chapter on the Typical Beauty of symmetry. Most of the writers apparently use the terms proportion and symmetry synonymously but Ruskin differentiated between these two terms of aesthetic order, *symmetry is the opposition of equal quantities of each other; proportion, the connection of unequal quantities with each other. The property of tree sending out equal boughs on opposite sides is symmetrical; its sending out shorter and smaller towards the top, proportional* (Works 4 : 125-26). Proportion, a relationship of changing and developing things, creates the unity of sequence while symmetry, which is static, creates opposition and balance.

Ruskin adds an Evengelical Anglican flavour to his Aristotlean sources, relating the beauty of symmetry to balance of divine justice and the right conduct among men. This same emphasis on order, appropriate and perhaps expectable in an aesthetic theory presented as a part of metaphysical appears in three remaining branches of Typical Beauty — repose, moderation and purity. Whereas unity amid variety, proportion, and symmetry are themselves the forms of order, repose and moderation are qualities produced by order or association with it. All art, says Ruskin, must have an element of repose may be *a simple appearance of permanence and quietness* (Works 4 : 114) or else it may be a repose proper, *the rest of things in which there is vitality or capability of motion actual or imagined* (Works 4 : 114). Repose could seem to answer yearning for peace, stability and order, both in life and art; *in architecture, in music, in acting, in dancing, in whatsoever art, great or mean there are yet degrees of greatness or meanness entirely dependent on this single quality of repose* (Works 4 : 119).

Ruskin believes that repose symbolises divine permanence, that aspect of God's nature which is in greatest contrast to the change and effort of human existence : *as opposed to passion, change, fulness or laborious exertion, Repose is the especial and separating characteristic of the internal mind and power. It is the "I am" of the Creator opposed to the "I became" of all creatures...it is the sign alike of the supreme volition which is incapable of change; it is the stillness of the beauty of the eternal chambers laid upon the variable waters ministering creatures* (Works 4 : 113).

Here peacefulness and permanence are the aspects of order which please by changing, changeable men, who always desire the calm of order. John D. Rosenberg has suggested that *in art or life he (Ruskin) was most moved by the kind of beauty which possessed the unchanging...remoteness of death* (203). This desire for repose enters both his aesthetics and critical practice, colouring his preference for subjects, who delighted in images of the eternal rest of men and mountains, intensely disliked portrayals of violence or violent emotions in art.

Purity, which less obviously partakes of Ruskin's emphasis upon order, is the type of divine energy, and its best example is light — *not all light, but light possessing the universal qualities of beauty, diffused or infinite rather than in points; tranquil, not startling and variable; pure, not sullied or oppressed* (Works 4 : 128).

Purity, referable to God, cannot mean singleness, because according to Ruskin, one cannot define God in negatives. He therefore explains that purity must signify some sort of energy, and from his remarks about the tranquil, constant nature of beautiful light it could appear that purity refers specifically to restrained divine energy. His preferences lead one visible embodiment of feeling, *the type of love* (Works 7 : 419), believes that internal colours which are more suitable convey the more emotional impression of a scene than do valient action or the depiction of faces under the influence of strong passions.

Nevertheless, as he explains in his chapter on moderation, the painter's colours, though intense, must avoid the glaring and discordant. Like all others aspects of painting, colour demands moderation, which Ruskin believes to be *the girdle and safeguard of all the rest, and in this respect the most essential of all* forms of beauty (Works 4 : 128). The appearance in material things of *self-restrained liberty* is beautiful, says Ruskin, because it is *the image of that acting of God with regard to all His creation, wherein, though free to operate in whatever arbitrary, sudden, violent, or inconstant ways He will, He yet, if we may reverently so speak, restrains is Himself, this His omnipotent liberty, and works always in consistent modes, called by us laws* (Works 4 : 138). Ruskin insists on the moral and artistic superiority of moderate things to *the loose, the lawless, the exaggerated, the insolent, and the profane* to things, to men, to colour, and forms which are disordered and hence unrelated to divine nature (Works 4 : 140). The general principle remains : all elements of painting, even colour which is the embodiment of feeling, require order and moderation.

After Ruskin has presented his theory Typical Beauty, he turns to the more emotional part of his aesthetic, Vital Beauty of living things. The theory of Vital Beauty which Ruskin presents, often puzzling, can better be understood, by continuing the contrast with Typical Beauty. If one relates both forms of beauty of Ruskin's metaphysics and religion, it will be seen that Typical Beauty is the beauty of forms and of certain qualities of forms, which Ruskin asserts to be aesthetically pleasing, because they represent and embody divine nature. Vital Beauty, on the other hand, is the beauty of living things and it is concerned not with forms but expression — with the expression of happiness and energy of life, and in a different manner, with the representation of moral truths by living things. In *Modern Painters Vol. II,* Ruskin introduces his theory of Vital Beauty. His states that it is *the appearance of felicitous fulfilment of function in living things, more especially of the joyful and right exertion of perfect life in man* (Works 4 : 64).

Man's function, is to glorify God by his obedience to God's law, which is consequently virtuous activity and hence productive of happiness; and by being happy man Ruskin means, beautiful. To create images of Vital Beauty in man, in painter must necessarily avoid depicting violent or debasing emotions. Ruskin, who desires something very much like a classical restraint in art, believed that, *the use and value of passion is not as a subject of contemplation in itself, but as, it breaks up the fountains of the great deep of human mind* (Works 4 : 204). Accepting emotionalist theories of art and moral perception, he emphasises that the painter should paint emotion to attain a further end, such as the rendering of character. Since he places such importance on the noble emotions, he despises a sensationalistic art which portrays violent passion only to titillate its audience, and in fact he hold that *all passion which attains overwhelming power is unfit for high art* (Works 4 : 204).

Ruskin's aesthetic theories are the product and type of irreconcilable dilemmas in his thoughts. When he wrote the second volume of *Modern Painters* he wished to take into account the subjective nature of beauty and yet make it a universal, objective phenomenon. Having begun with the premise that emotion is the basis of art, beauty and morality, he wished to avoid the disordering as well as the subjective nature of emotion. And, arguing from the principle that the physical, the material, is only dross, he wished to show that the beauty of physically existing things is of greater value than the things themselves.

In his recent anthology *Ruskin Today,* Sir Kenneth Clark comments that *no other writer, perhaps, has suffered so great a fall in reputation as Ruskin* (xiii), and one might well add that his philosophy of beauty has more than any other part of his work, been neglected and has lost prestige it once enjoyed. Joan Evans, who has contributed a biography, dismisses these theories of beauty almost without discussion. Quentin Bell, author of a recent study of Ruskin's life and works, considers the volume that contains the burden of his aesthetic speculation to be a matter of *splendid inconsequences* (21).

More than a century after he first became known to the British public, his reputation is again on the rise, though, often one must admit, for reasons that would have pained him. He hated to be considered a mere world painter, yet Evans considers his great merit to lie in the fact that he was an *artist in words* (87).

To regard him only as an artist in words is to ignore Ruskin's value both his own time and to ours; it is to suggest most erroneously that we have nothing to learn from his writings, and his questions no longer interest us because we have answered them. Such complacency and lack of curosity hardly became an age whose art, whose general surroundings, Ruskin has so affected. Peter Quenell rightly remarks : *...he did his best to open his audience's eyes to an unknown world of beauty* (16). In aesthetic theory, Ruskin, is seen by Hugh Walker as *Newman of the aesthetic movement* (712). Like Newman he was repelled by the pure rationalism of the 18th century. René Wellek's remark about Ruskin's aesthetic theory is highly valuable : *Ruskin's significance in literary criticism is not due to any of his scattered opinions or comments, rather...due to his aesthetics* (137).

WORKS CITED

Ball, A.H.R., ed., *Ruskin as a Literary Critic : Selections*, Cambridge : Cambridge University Press, 1928.

Bell, Quentin, *Ruskin*, Ediburgh/London : np, 1963.

Clark, Sir Kenneth, *Ruskin Today*, London : np, 1964.

Evans, Joan, *John Ruskin,* London : np, 1954.

Harding, J.D., *The Principles and Practice of Art*, London : np, 1845.

Landow, George P., *Aesthetics and the Critical Theories of Ruskin*, Princeton : Princeton UP, 1971.

Quenell, Peter, "John Ruskin" in *Bibliographical Series : Writers and Their Works*, No. 76, np : Longman, 1956.

Rosenberg, John D., *The Darkening Glass : A Portrait of Ruskin's Genius*, New York/London : np, 1961.

Ruskin, John, *The Complete Works of John Ruskin,* 39 vols, Eds. E.T. Cook and Alexander Wedderburn, London : np, 1903-12.

Walker, Hugh, *The Literature of the Victorian Era*, Delhi : np, 1955.

Wellek, René, *A History of Modern Criticism,* Vol. 3, Cambridge : np, 1983.

4

Library Criticism and Aesthetics

—*Sushma Sharma*

IT is, indeed, the primary duty of a critic of life to have endeavoured hard to get at the springs of life and to identify its natural temper with what goes on around us, and to identify himself with it. It is, however, notable that the creator of literature is also duty bound to create. As a result of his artistic imagination, his experiences of life, his gift of representation and his desire to offer a semblance of life, all combined to produce such a work of art as delights the reader or the spectator. The artist or the creator of life is also supposed to create a beautiful picture which presupposes a thorough imaginative assimilation as well as the function of the accredited technique of artistic creation, A poet or a dramatist is concerned with grasping the truth of life in such way as to attract the attention of the reader or the spectator to something beautiful. Coleridge, a great romantic poet, who is also a great literary romantic critic has aptly emphasized the fact that a piece of art is something not only less than a reality, it is also more than a reality.

Reality is a simple fact which is tempered into beautiful with the help of the aspects of the different forms of craftsmanship. This is called aesthetics *i.e.* the rendering of life into a beautiful piece of art. That beauty has its own power to inspire, to charm, to exhort and to encourage. An aesthete, while he is a creator of life basically, is also a creator of beauty called the literary or the artistic beauty. The different literateurs, poets and dramatists and prose writers have had the different stamps of the temper and the culture of their own times went a long way to create beauty consonant probably with what was expected during the period, *e.g.* the Romanticists have their own way to approach life; their own paraphernalia employed for the purpose.

In the eighteenth century they employed the means available at the time for the creation of beauty; in the Romantic period they were guided by a different vision; the Victorians looked at a different form, and wrested beauty out of it with the means at their command. In the twentieth century they are employing their own ways and approaching objects thereby creating beauty in unforeseen ways.

To begin with, it is advisable for us to examine the place and the temper of the time to which Longinus belongs before passing the verdict as to his being a critic of life and an aesthete.

Criticism, ordinarily speaking, implies an appreciation of a thing. Literary criticism implies the appreciation of a piece of literature, a poem, a play or an other form of literature in prose or verse. Literature, as a piece of art is the result of an imaginative endeavour to see life. By seeing life we mean the understanding of life in its true and real perspective, by showing life we mean an effective expression of what a literary artist has been able to see out of life.

All art is the imitation of life. Literature is a form of life, and as such, it is also an imitation of life. It is in other words, the imaginative reconstruction of those phases of life which significantly strike the notice of the literary artist. It conveys the seeing, the impressions or the ideas of that portion of life which he has been able to assimilate and which he can claim as his own. In a word, it is his own criticism of life.

The aim and function of a critic, should be visualized in view of the above. While a poet deals with life itself, a literary critic deals with the imaginative reconstruction of life. Thus, while the material of creative artist is life itself, the material of the literary critic is the representation or the recreation of life, that is, a piece of art. It will not be wrong to assert that while a creative art is a criticism of life, criticism is the criticism of the criticism of life. The creative artist understands, interprets and exposes life; the literary critic understands, interprets and exposes the piece of art.

We take it for granted that a creative writer is gifted with a special natural gift of sensibility coupled with an intellectual and emotional culture. Similarly, we also accept that a literary critic is endowed with a power of sensibility which is above that of average men and women, and also an intellectual culture which stands him in good stead in his duty as a literary critic. Imagination, of course, is the very creative faculty which is indispensable both to the creative artist and the critic. Over and above these gifts of artistic sensibility and imagination, a literary writer is supposed to have looked long and deeply into life. He is supposed to have reaped his own experience from his first-hand observation of the varied phenomena of life. And this is not all. He is expected not only to have studied the book of life widely and intelligently but also to have imbibed the very spirit of the complexes thereof. It is also presumed that the author has made his own at least that portion of life which he artistically communicates. In the same way we look for a certain amount of culture, literary and intellectual, on the part of the critic. When we approach a critic with faith, we believe that the critic must have studied widely and intelligently. We also believe that he has imbibed the real spirit of the literature or literatures which he has studied and appreciated. His material being literature itself, it is natural to accept that he is the master of a literary acumen and insight, which are remarkable in their degree. It is also presumed that a literary critic is happily gifted with a knack for discrimination and categorization, for otherwise, he would not be able to juxtapose the different forms of literature under their respective categories.

The intellectual and artistic culture will be of little account until and unless the critic has an atmosphere of mental purity, which may also be called imaginative purity. Here we come face to face with a very grave problem of literary criticism. Our experience tells us that quite a number of critics have approached literature with a mind which is already stuffed with prejudices in favour or against their subject. This is highly undesirable, rather detrimental to criticism. Matthew Arnold, one of the greatest modern critics of English Literature lays down that the major function of criticism is to discover and to propagate the best that has been produced anywhere in the world. Let the critics range be ever limited to one or two literatures, his function is to discover the best that has ever been created. How on earth can he really discover the best if his critical vision is not unaffected; if it is already blurred and distorted by his own preconceived notion or notions? It is imperative, therefore, on the part of a literary critic, in the same way as on the part of a creative writer, to be detached in his attitude to his material. If he allows his own bias to come forth in the way of this own critical endeavour, he will not be able to do his duty as a critic. He will not be able to reveal to the lovers of literature the best treasures of literary beauty and power that the piece of literature contains. He will fail to guide those who depend upon his honest endeavour and his literary insight. On the other hand, he will stand as an impediment, as a substantial obstruction in the way of a reader who had better been left alone under these circumstances, to make use of his own literary resources independently.

When we talk of criticism, we presuppose that it is unaffected and unspoiled by any bias whatever. We presuppose that the critic is imbued happily with a comprehensive sense of responsibility, with a comprehensive intellectual and artistic culture, gifted with an uncommon artistic sensibility, possessed of strength enough not to be swayed by any prejudice or unhealthy complex. Such a critic is on sure grounds. He is fit to serve the cause of literature as he is expected to do. He will be able to expose and interpret literature, as he is alive, all the time, to the beauties, the graces and the power of the piece of literature.

Criticism, thus, renders definite service to literature and the lovers of literature. In the light of the above Longinus who is called the first romantic critic may be fully and fairly examined.

From Aristotle to Longinus there is a gap of several centuries. Longinus was divinely chosen to sound a great truth in his "Essay on the Sublime". With his rare literary insight and clear aesthetic vision he was able to probe deep into the problems of literature. He could well discern in what the real power of literature lies. He stressed unmistakably that the function of art is not only to persuade and delight but also to transport, to lift one out of oneself into the realms of sublimity.

There is a still unsettled controversy about the time to which Longinus belonged. While some critics lay stress on his belonging to the first century A.D., the others and a larger number of critics including Scott James opine that Longinus who rendered yeoman's service to the Queen of Zenobia belongs to the third century A.D. However, we are not very particular about his distinction. What concerns us more is the contribution he made to the discovery of the best for the development of the literary criticism, and a free and sure appreciation of what constitutes the beauty and dignity of a piece of art.

Writing to one of his friends, Terentianus Longinus says : "Sublimity is a certain distinction and excellence in expression and it is from no other source than this that the greatest poets and writers have derived eminence and gained an immortality of renown. The effect of elevated language upon audience is not persuasion but transport."

The definition of the sublime as given by Longinus is a very appropriate one. He calls it an 'echo of the soul' for, the sublime consists in a certain loftiness and perfection of language. A great work of art startles us. Longinus believes that the sublime at the critical moment shoots forth and tears the whole thing in pieces like a thunderbolt and in a flash reveals all the writer's powers.

One finds the perception and nature of the sources of the sublime properly explained. He says that there are five principal sources of alleviated language; the first and the most important is the power of forming great conceptions. Secondly, there is vehement and inspired passion. These two components of the subtle are for the most part innate. Those which remain are partly the product of art, two sorts of figures, both of thought and of expression. The next is noble diction, which in turn comprises choice of words, and use of metaphors and elaboration of language. The fifth, cause of elevation, one feels is the fitting conclusion of all that have preceded. It is dignified and elevated composition. He also brings out the distinction between the real sublime and the false sublime. Some writers employ stale expression which is highly turgid. It is not real sublime which is not, indeed, the echo of the soul. Longinus freely and emphatically exhorts writers to guard themselves against such a manner as he calls false sublime.

Another virtue which can be assigned to the credit of Longinus lies in the fact that he asserted the importance of comparative criticism, with the help of comparative literature he either bore a contrast between the two or more literatures, or explained their respective value and achievements. He compared the orators and writers living in different countries at the same time. He also compared the work of writers living in the classical or post classical period. Thus, he throws a flood of light on the merits and success thereof in the case of different periods.

The greatness of Longinus lies in the fact that he approaches his work impartially and enlightens the reader with a more intelligent appreciation. His interpretations anticipate modern criticism, for, in them he laid emphasis upon the appreciation of the essence of literature, on the beauty of words and the aesthetic value of literature.

Criticism is a very healthy artistic activity, which partakes of the intellectual, emotional and aesthetic achievement of a writer, a writer who creates, particularly the literature of power as emphasized by De Quincy. It is really creditable that in the early period when the seeds of intellectual and aesthetic culture were being sown, Longinus was capable of catching the glimpse of the heavenly light which found its reflection in the creation of the literature of power.

A close study of Plato's works gives one to understand that Plato's thesis runs into two currents : the philosophical which was carried forward by Plotinus and the aesthetic which constituted the mainstay of Longinus's critical activity. The students of literary criticism are happy to find that Longinus was able to catch the light of the great truth that the real function of the literature of power lies in its ability to transport man's mind into regions unknown. It may be particularly noted that Longinus was free entirely from any prejudicial approach or propaganda. His aim was simply and primarily to get at the light which constitutes the real power of literary art; and he was, indeed, able to get at it, not only to get at it but also to communicate it with an artistic tenderness. Not only Vincent Smith, but Matthew Arnold and Scott James have also concurred in conceding to Longinus a place of meritorious achievement. His treatise 'On the Sublime' is unquestionably an unflinching achievement in the right direction, and offers a solid guidance which will invariably put the lovers of art in a good stead to approach a piece of art and enable him to catch the light and dignity.

Among the critics of literature Longinus enjoys a distinguished place for his yeoman's service rendered to the development of literary criticism. Previously art was looked upon as an effective means of delight and exhortation. An indication of the great beauty and power of literary art was hurled inadvertently by Plato, who recommended the banishment of poets and poetry from the state of Athens which he aimed at seeing growing into an ideal state. Plato conceived that an ideal state is one where people, in all their thought and actions are guided by reason.

Longinus also realized the real power of poetry, but he did consider it to be a political or cultural bane. He found in the great power of art a natural power and beauty which ennobles the human spirit. His realization of the real power of poetry, his realization of the genuine service rendered by language and figures of speech in the attainment of the sublime, his clear distinction drawn between the Real and the False subtle in order to open before the poetic aspirants the new vista for their artistic and imaginative creation — all these have immortalized

Longinus as one of the greatest critics of literary art, but particularly poetry. It is he who offered to the English romantic poets like Wordsworth, Shelley, Keats the light that enabled them to make great achievement in the realm of poetry.

5

The Legacy of the 'Appropriator'

—Sukriti Ghosal

THE critical theories of Oscar Wilde are generally underrated for being thoroughly derivative. In reviewing *Intentions,* the volume of major critical essays by Wilde, Arthur Symons ironically remarks that Wilde 'is always original in his quotations' (*CH* 96). Whistler's verdict is that Wilde 'has the courage of the opinions — of others' (*SL* 66). This view that Wilde is but a witty synthesizer of other men's ideas, has even been endorsed by Prof. René Wellek to whom Wilde, despite his brilliance, is but a 'propagandist for ideas of his predecessors' *(HMC* 409). True, Wilde came under the influence of many of his critical predecessors, especially Arnold and Pater. But my contention is that, notwithstanding his notoriety as a critical plagiarist, as a theorist Wilde is original enough to influence his critical epigones.

A plausible psychological interpretation of this attitude is in terms of 'the anxiety of influence'. Harold Bloom demonstrates how strong poets, compelled to define their own originality against the overriding achievement of their predecessors, suffer from 'anxiety of indebtedness' (*AI* 5) which often manifests itself in the form of deliberate misreading of their precursors. For most modern critics, such an 'anxious (involuntary) reaction' to Wilde seems unlikely because to the late 20th century critics Wilde is but part of a tradition. Incidentally, ideas imbibed from a tradition are not generally treated as influence, for the term at least partly 'conceals and mitigates the guilty acquisition of talent' (*ED* 3). However, in T.S. Eliot there is much uneasy reaction to Wilde probably because most of his critical dicta have been drawn upon Wilde's ideas.

Specks of influential anxiety and consequent intentional misreading are too conspicuous in Eliot to be overlooked. In his essay 'Arnold and Pater', by way of defining aestheticism Eliot observes : 'If we wish to understand painting, we do not go to Oscar Wilde' (*SE* 400). In the same essay Eliot sneeringly mentions Wilde's *De Profundis* as a work exemplifying the objectionable equation of Religion and Art, an equation inspired by Arnold's theory of culture which strips religion of faith. However, Eliot's theoretical dismissal of Wilde is belied by his critical practice where he appropriates many of Wilde's seminal ideas oftener than known. The idea of tradition is undeniably the cornerstone of Eliotean aesthetics. Tradition, according to Eliot, involves a 'historical sense' — 'a perception, not only of the pastness of the past but its presence' (*SE* 14). Eliot criticises the defiance of convention in the name of originality and asserts that the best part of a work is that 'in which the dead poets...assert their immortality most vigorously' (*SE* 14). Eliot here but smartly rephrases Wilde's insistence on the artist's having, supratemporal consciousness :

> ...he to whom the present is the only thing that is present knows nothing of the age in which he lives. To realize the nineteenth century, one must realize every century that has preceded it and that has contributed to its making (*CW* 1040).

Again, Wilde stresses the importance of critical faculty in creation :

> For it is critical faculty that invents fresh forms. The tendency of creation is to repeat itself.... The mere creative instinct does not innovate, but reproduces (*CW* 1021).

Eliot too asserts that if tradition is nothing better than blind adherence to what has gone before, it should positively be discouraged : '...novelty is better than repetition' (*SE* 14). The phrasal affinity is too close to be merely adventitious.

As a critic Eliot espouses the impersonality of art emotions and emphasizes the need for alchemizing personal emotions into poetic artifacts :

> Impressions and experiences which are important for the man may take no place in the poetry, and those which become important in the poetry may play quite a negligible part in the man, personality (*SE* 20).

Wilde's view in this regard is so strikingly identical with Eliot's that the latter seems to have used the former as his main source. In his Preface to *The Picture of Dorian Gray* Wilde presents his view epigrammatically : 'To reveal art and conceal the artist is art's aim' (*CW* 17). In 'The Soul of Man Under Socialism' he spells out his conviction about the impersonality of art emotion more wittily :

> To call an artist morbid because he deals with morbidity as his subject matter is as silly as if one called Shakespeare mad because he wrote *King Lear (CW* 1093).

It is interesting to note that Eliot through his catalyst — analogy argues for absolute, even mechanical, impersonality of treatment. Wilde, however, has the critical sanity to see that impersonality is at best 'intellectual'. Since art springs from personality, the most impersonal characters, he rightly maintains, are 'the poets themselves not *as they thought they were,* but *as they thought they, were not'* (*CW* 1045). Since 'out of ourselves we can never pass', 'the man who suffers and the mind which creates', *pace* Eliot, can never be 'completely separate' even in the most perfect artist, except, of course, in some wished — for way.

Ian Small in an article shows that in modern criticism one finds an increasing attenuation of the representational values of art : 'the more modernist a text, the more self-consciously artefactual it is' (*BJA* 50). The text is no longer looked upon as a transparent glass-window opening on reality but rather as a stained glass, 'meant to be looked *at,* rather than *through*' (*ICCT* 12). Almost a century before this we find Wilde contesting the reflective theory of art in 'The Decay of Lying' : 'Art finds her own perfection within, and not outside of, herself.... She is a veil rather than a mirror' (*CW* 982). In a letter to More Adey he further claims that 'Art is not a mirror but a crystal. It creates its own shapes and forms' (*SL* 415). Modern art, again, is not an art of vision, but rather an art of revision. W.B. Yeats, like Flaubert, is unwilling to take the poet as an inspired author transcribing telepathically the aesthetic dictations of the Muse. In his poem 'Adam's Curse' he beautifully verbalises this modernist postulate with a metaphor of stitching :

> A line will take us hours maybe;
> Yet if it does not seem a moment's thought,
> Our stitching and unstitching has been naught.

Long before Yeats Wilde would dislodge the inspirational theory of literary creation. He strongly holds that 'practice must precede perfection' (*CW* 972) and reminds us that 'there are moments when Art almost attains to the dignity of manual labour' (*CW* 220).

As a theorist T.S. Eliot endeavours to shift the critical focus from the poet to the work. In the Preface to the 1928 edition of *The Sacred Wood,* he asserts that 'a poem, in some sense has its own life; ...that the feeling, or emotion, or vision resulting from a poem is something different from the feeling or emotion or vision in the mind of the poet' (*SW* x). The critical premise involved here has long been anticipated by Wilde :

> For when a work is finished it has, as it were, an independent life of its own, and may deliver a message far other than that which was put into its lips to say (*CW* 1024).

It's a pity that J.C. Ransom traces this New Critical idea to Richards and Eliot but ignores Wilde who, however, had fought for views by which Eliot won a name for himself.

Wilde's, and later Eliot's, suggestion that a poem may imply something unintended by the poet, contains the seed of the 'intentional fallacy' propounded by Wimsatt and Beardsley. They argue that since 'the design or intention of the author is neither available nor desirable as a standard' for judging his literary merit, what the poet set out to do is immaterial (*TCLC* 334). There is an unambiguous prefiguration of this critical principle in *Intentions*. In 'The Critic as Artist' Wilde avers that criticism does not confine itself 'to discovering the real intention of the artist and accepting that as final' (*CW* 1029). That this is not just a passing remark is evident from what he further notes in *De Profundis* written three years before his death : 'in art good intentions are not of the smallest value. All bad art is the result of good intentions' (*SL* 223).

The dynamics of Wilde criticism also embodies some of the basic Post-Structuralist doctrines. The New Critics while questioning the authorial intention, read the text in terms of fixed formula — be it of 'irony', 'paradox' (Wimsatt) or 'ambiguity' (Empson) or 'tension' (Tate). However ingenious the interpretation, each of these approaches reduces the 'heterogeneity of texts into a version of the author's (complex) self' (*PD* 6), what R.S. Crane describes as the 'bankruptcy of critical monism'. Eminent Post-Structuralists like Roland Barthes, therefore speak about the 'irreducible' plurality of signification (*RL* 53-54). Strange though it may sound, we find a clear anticipation of this unorthodox view of interpretation in the writings of Oscar Wilde. In 'The Critic as Artist' he states that to the critic art is not the 'riddling Sphinx' whose questions may be answered. It rather is an undecipherable mystery, a mode of expression whose imaginative beauty makes all interpretations true, and no interpretation final' (*CW* 1031). Wilde here accepts music as 'the perfect type of art', for its 'secret' is inexhaustible, and concludes : 'It is through its very incompleteness that Art becomes complete in beauty' (*CW* 1031).

Another significant change found in Post-Structuralist poetics is the primacy of the reader. Pre-modern aesthetics is too much author-centred. The filial obligation is so strong here that most critics fret themselves sick to grasp the author's meaning. In modern poetics the attention veers from the author to the work. But in Post-Structuralist critical theory the thrust swerves to the reader. The Post-Structuralists think that unlike a work which has a spatial existence, a text is a methodological field which emerges only when the work comes in contact with the reader's consciousness. The reader's role here is pivotal, for he is not to consume the text but to produce or co-author the text (*RL* 54). The reader, thus, becomes the true author of this joint construct. Even in respect of the reader's pre-eminence in the generation of meaning, Wilde pioneers the modern critics. In 'The Critic as Artist' he first puts his point tentatively : '...the meaning of any beautiful created thing is, at least, as much in the soul of him who looks at it as it was in his soul who wrought it'. Then modifying his opinion he makes a claim untypical of a Victorian: 'Nay, it is rather the beholder who lends to the beautiful thing its myriad meanings and makes it marvellous for us...' (*CW* 1029). The emphasis-switch, which struck the Victorians as preposterous convinces us of the profundity of Wilde's critical insight which has taken about a century to be formulated into a theory.

Evidently, Oscar Wilde is not an 'intellectual of attitudes' (*SOW* 47) or an eccentric theorist who delights in juggling with critical platitudes. True, his style is too repetitive, too digressive, too elusive. But a serious reading of his criticism will reveal that Oscar Wilde is seldom wayward in his judgement. Wilde's critical principles are always well ahead of his time and far from being an appropriator, he is the fountainhead of many key-tenets of modern criticism.

WORKS CITED

Barry, Peter (ed.), *Issues in Contemporary Critical Theory*, A Casebook, London : Macmillan, 1987. Cited as *ICCT*.

Barthes, Roland, *The Rustle of Language,* trans. Richard Howard, Oxford : Basil Blackwell, 1986. Cited as *RL*.

Beckson, Karl (ed.), *Oscar Wilde : The Critical Heritage*, London : Routledge and Kegan Paul, 1970, Cited as *CH*.

Bloom, Harold., *The Anxiety of Influence : A Theory of Poetry*, New York : Oxford University Press, 1973. Cited as *AI*.

Easthope, Antony, *Poetry as Discourse*, London : Methuen, 1983. Cited as *PD*.

Eliot, T.S., *The Sacred Wood : Essays on Poetry and Criticism*, 1920; rpt. London : Methuen, 1960. Cited as *SW*.

Eliot, T.S., *Selected Essays*, London : Faber and Faber, 1932. Cited as *SE*.

Ellmann, Richard, *Eminent Domain*, New York : Oxford University Press, 1964. Cited as *ED*.

Hart-Davis, Rupert (ed.), *Selected Letters of Oscar Wilde*, Oxford : Oxford, 1979. Cited as *SL*.

Lodge, David (ed.), *Twentieth Century Literary Criticism : A Reader*, 1972; rpt. London : Longman. 1985, Cited as *TCLC*.

Small, Ian, 'Semiotics and Oscar Wilde's Accounts of Art', *British Journal of Aesthetics*, 25, No. 1 (Winter 1985). Cited as *BJA*.

Symons, Arthur, *A Study of Oscar Wilde*, London : Charles J. Sawyer, 1930. Cited as *SOW*.

Wellek, René, *A History of Modern Criticism 1750-1950*, IV, New Haven : Yale University Press, 1983. Cited as *HMC*.

Wilde, Oscar, *The Complete Works of Oscar Wilde*, intr. Vyvyan Holland, 1948; rpt. London : Collins, 1983. Cited as *CW*.

6

The Concept of Imagination in I.A. Richards

—*Anjani Kumar*

IMAGINATION is derived from Latin Imagatio, which was a late substitute for phantasia (a simple transliteration of the Greek from which fancy is derived). The two terms with their derivatives, long appeared as synonyms designating the image-receiving or image-forming faculty or process. From Philosophy, they were borrowed by criticism and in both contexts were subject to different evaluations by different schools from the platonic point of view, the image is confined to appearance and opinion.

The intellectual and emotional climate of our time has something to do with the characteristic development of literary criticism in the present age. Victorian poetic conventions and theories had become outmoded in the context of the development of semantics, symbolic logic, cultural anthropology and the psychology of Jung and Freud.

In developing his strategy as a new apologist for poetry, Richards seems to have absorbed the influence of the researches of non-metaphysical philosophy and especially those of the logic of science of the early decades of the present century. Richards reacted sharply against the tendency of the transcendentalist to mystify imagination. He affirms in this context "There is nothing peculiarly mysterious about imagination. It is no more marvelous than any other of the ways of the mind" (Richards 191).

In his desire to avoid part of the fate, which befell Coleridge, Richards develops a cautious approach to the problem of imagination. His account of imagination, he claims, will be devoid of theological implications. The luminous hints dropped by Coleridge in his description of the primary imagination as the living power and the prime Agent of all human perception seems to have dazzled and perplexed succeeding speculators. With the aid of some active impulses others are aroused in the absence of what would otherwise be their necessary stimuli. Richards calls such impulses imaginative, whether images occur or not. He does not regard image production as an essential part of the imaginative process. In the original non-imaginary experience of the poet, certain impulses, aroused by their necessary stimuli, co-operate together. In the imaginary experience of the reader or the auditor, certain impulses are aroused even in the absence of the necessary stimuli. Imagination is considered as such combination or fusion of mental elements as resulted in certain valuable states of mind and fancy was regarded as a mere trivial playing with these elements.

Richards developed a profound interest in his theory of imagination. He was particularly attracted towards Coleridge. He describes *Biographia Literaria* as "the lumber room of neglected wisdom" (Richards 193).

The impact of Coleridge's thought on Richards in pervasive, complicated and subtle. "The development of Richards's books" as Hyman wilily puts, it is the "reads like thc record of a love affair" (331).

In *Coleridge on Imagination,* Richards presents a detailed examination of the Coleridgean distinction between "Fancy" and 'Imagination" and builds up his own theory of Imagination as re-interpretation and as an assimilation of the Coleridgean theory. Richards contends that an observable and definable difference between "Fancy" and "Imagination" is the central point of Coleridge's critical theory. As a psychologist, Coleridge made a careful distinction between "Fancy" and "Imagination" which to him were "too distinct and widely different faculties, instead of being according to the general belief, either two names with one meaning or at furthest, the lower and higher degree of one and the same power". Richards contends that in distinguishing betweèn the various modes of combination of different distinguishable types of mental activity, we have to repeat Coleridge's words. "The poet, described an ideal perfection, brings the whole soul of man into activity, with the subordination of its faculties to one another according to their relative worth and dignity."

In expounding Coleridge's 'Theory of Imagination' Richards starts, like Coleridge, with a theory of the act of knowledge, or of consciousness or in Coleridgean terms, with the coincidence or coalescence of an object with a subject, Richards introduces some of the technical terms which Coleridge used to develop his Schellingean conception of mind. "Coalescence of subject and object" explains the working of the "Imagination". To understand this coalescence we must use "Philosophy" whose method is the inner sense "Coleridge's subject is the self or the intelligence, the sentient knowing mind his object is nature, what known by the mind in the act of knowing. As Richards shrewdly notes, Coleridge's subject-object machinery introduces no split between the ingredients of the mind. A constructing, forming activity from the mind has entered into the simplest, seeming datum. And the perceiving and the forming are the same. The subject has gone into what it perceives, and what perceives is, in the sense, itself. So the object becomes the subject, and the subject, the object.

Richards finds valuable basis for his theory in Coleridge's separation of a primary from a secondary Imagination. Richards finds a equivalent for the primary Imagination in normal perception that produces the usual word of the senses. The secondary Imagination reforming this world infuses it with poetry and every aspect of the routine world in which it is invested with other values than those necessary for bare continuance as living beings. Both primary and secondary Imaginations are vital, in contrast to the mechanical power of, Fancy, which merely collects and re-arranges, without re-making them, units of meaning already produced by the creative, growing power of Imagination. In Imagination, the mind is growing, in Fancy it is merely reassembling products of its past creation, stereotyped as objects.

In the concept of Imagination I.A. Richards has analysed the doctrines of Coleridge and Locke with a view to exhibiting, them in common terms. His aim is to discover what each is doing and to find out a means of comparing their doings. In this way, a common framework may be found in which the rival speculative machineries can be examined.

Richards perceptively notes that here the several units of meaning surrender almost all their local independence in common co-operative purpose. At several places Richards has translated Coleridge's way of discussing "Fancy" and "Imagination" in the terms which might sometimes have been repugnant as suggesting mechanical treatment to Coleridge himself.

According to Richards Imagination sets off a sort of effortless, exhilarating continuing activity of the mind. He seems to treat it as a hallmark of the Imagination. He sanctions the process by describing it as "living" and "growing". In responding to an imaginative passage, we are invited to stretch our minds, and one can flatter himself that he has ever finished the process of understanding.

Ranson asserts that nobody is better entitled than Richards to the honour of being the discoverer of the importances of irrelevance in poetry. Indeed for Richards, the distinguishing work of Imagination is very much in terms of relevance.

Richards widens the application of the concept of Fancy and Imagination to literary genre, outside poetry and applies it particularly to works of fiction. The conception of Imagination was used by Coleridge as a means of describing the wider and deeper powers of some poetry. Richards takes it as a descriptive psychological term in the sense that it points facts which explain certain values under the checks of the senses and reason, of the activity of thought and the vivacity of the accumulated memory. The exercise of the Imagination is for Coleridge, more valuable than the operations of Fancy. By relaxing the condition, Richards seeks to make the terms purely descriptive. Coleridge says "Good sense is the Body of poetic genius, Fancy its Drapery, Motion its life and Imagination the soul, that is everywhere, and in each and forms all into a graceful and intelligent whole." Richards comments that this is a peroration in an 18th century manner, not designed to be taken seriously.

Cleanth Brooks in his review of *Coleridge on Imagination* commends Richards for his defense of the validity of Coleridge's famous distinction between the Fancy and Imagination.

The Wind Harp image in *The Dejection Ode* refers to the poetic process in its highest imaginative intensity. It is Richards's contention that the Wind-Harp image (the language of poetry) can achieve the coalescence of the two doctrines.

In *The boundaries of the Mythical*, Richards finds the key to the solution of the conflict between science and value in terms of the different senses attached to the term 'Nature'. The Platonic doctrine of ideas is useful to him in this context. Richards accepts the Coleridgean theory of Imagination but divests it of its transcedental mysticism.

Coleridge on Imagination has vital link with Richards early writings and we should not miss these links. "Richards has re-ordered an important conception of Imagination and crowned it" (424).

Richards vindicates the tremendous powers of Imagination by crowning it as a sovereign creative principle. To put the point more effectively Richards cites the following lines from Yeats's *Among school children.*

O. body swayed to music
O. brightening glance

How can we know the dancer from the dance?

This unity of content and form, of spirit and letter, of intuition and expression, is, of course, a perennial theme of criticism and of poetry itself. Poetry exemplifies this interdependence in this unity. Coleridge's organic conception of poetry is thus re-stated by Richards in the modern idiom and Coleridge's concept of Imagination receives a modern realistic and naturalistic re-interpretation in Richards's critical writings.

WORKS CITED

Blackmur, R.P., In *The Nation*, April 10, 1935.

Hyman, Stanley Edgar, *The Armed Vision : A Study in the Methods of Modern Literary Criticism*, New York : Knopf, 1948, Revised Edition, 1955.

Richards, I.A., *Principles of Literary Criticism*, London : Paul Trench Trubner, 1924. New York : Hartcourt Brace, 1925, Eighth Impression, 1945.

7

R.S. Crane : A Neo-Aristotelian

—Asit Biswas

DURING the thirties and early forties of the twentieth century the major "controversy among literary theorists centred chiefly on the 'true' nature of poetry and the 'proper' character of criticism" (Crane *Preface,* iii). I do not want to generalize or oversimplify the complex critical scene of the thirties and early forties. But truly speaking that was, in brief, what the critics of this transitional period had been trying to achieve. The traditions of impressionistic and moralistic criticisms were already estimated to be incomplete and unsatisfactory. The primary enthusiasm of Marxist Criticism was also at a low ebb. The new trend in criticism initiated by Eliot and Richards reached its height in the New Criticism. But it has also failed to offer us a method of comprehensive criticism of literary art. Different critics of this group tend to give us different views of poetry and poetic criticism. In such a situation the writings of the Chicago group of critics received some attention. Their primary aim was to rectify the deficiencies of all the previous critical theories and to offer a scientific and fruitful method for critical analysis. They do not discard any theory as wrong. They examine the limitations of the past theories — their tendencies of dogmatism and reductionism — and emphasize the necessity of formulating a really fruitful method of critical judgment on the basis of a knowledge of the defects of the preceding theories. Eliseo Vives, in his review of *Critics and Criticism*, has rightly observed that "Crane and his friends have always put main emphasis on the principles and methods of criticism" (Vives 137). And the way they followed for a comprehensive critical analysis and evaluation of literally texts very soon made them known as 'neo-Aristotelians'. Kenneth Burke in 1945 dubbed them so in his book *A Grammar of Motives*. The Chicago critics themselves hardly approved of this title and registered repeated protests in their writings. Still they continue to be called neo-Aristotelians, and not without reason.

To a Chicago critic a poem or a literary work is a distinctive whole which has its own unique function in human experience. And also, criticism to them is a reasoned discourse. Both the concepts make the Chicagoans Aristotelian in some respect. Crane himself admits in his 'Preface' to *Critics and Criticism* that Aristotle is actually there "behind what they [the Chiago critics] have sought to do in many of their essays in poetic theory and practical criticism" (Crane, *Preface,* iv). This statement marks Crane and his followers as essentially neo-Aristotelian.

But I must hasten to add that Crane is a neo-Aristotelian in a very limited sense. It, by no way, means that he is a dogmatic supporter of Aristotle and his approach. Crane has clearly said that they have been "greatly interested, all along, in the particular class of critical problems which Aristotle was the first, possibly the last, to discuss systematically, and for the study of which he evolved an appropriate and workable method" (Crane, *Preface,* iii). And, therefore, they tried to "pursue similar lines of study in the poetics of modern literature" (Crane, *Preface,* iii). They have thus enlarged and modified the Aristotelian approach through additions and alterations in the light of the literary needs of the century. They never support Aristotle blindly. They are, thus, 'neo-Aristotelian' in a very restricted sense. Crane's "our loyalty at any rate should be to problems rather than to ancient masters" (Crane, *Languages of Criticism*, 149) sounds like a warning to themselves and to the succeeding generations of critics. In other words, Crane warns us against a dogmatic following of Aristotle. At the same time he suggests that we should not hesitate to take help of his insights if we find that they may enable us to solve the problems we face in an analysis and understanding of literary texts. It will almost be the same as our contemporary critics benefit from the observations of Freud, Jung, Frazer and such others. The Chicagoans, it is remarkable, oppose some earlier Aristotelians who sought to extend Aristotle's observations on tragedy to other literary genres. The Chicagoans stand aloof from this group due to their belief, in a purely Aristotelian strain, that "each literary genre has its own principles of construction, and poems achieve wholeness by conforming to the principles of their genres" (Pritchard 281).

Crane's close association with Aristotle is evident from his practice both as a literary theoretician and as a practical critic. Aristotle, unlike almost any other philosopher considering poetic art seriously, believed in a theory of the multiplicity of linguistic systems. Plato, for instance, used the same system of language for the discussion of both poetry and music. He of course treated the two subjects differently, but the language of his discussion is essentially the same. Other philosophers like Hume, Hobbes, Hegel and Croce also take help more or less of a single language to discuss both poetry and other arts in themselves as well as in relation to other things. But Aristotle believed that every distinguishable thing, such as poetry, presents a multiplicity of aspects and relations, each one of which may be examined in different languages or critical frameworks. And in his own practice Aristotle is found to use different system of language and principles for talking about poetry, for example, in his different treatises — on poetry, on ethics, on politics and the like. Thus, while in politics Aristotle is concerned with efficient causes in relation to the good of citizens, in Poetics it is the intrinsic good in relation to the art of the poet. It will be a mistake, Crane warns, to understand and consider them in the same way. The validity of a statement can be determined only by its proper contextualization.

Crane explains the major assumptions upon which Aristotle bases the line of inquiry he pursues in the *Poetics*, and these assumptions, Crane thinks, give him the basic framework of his analysis. Naturally, the critical propositions which Aristotle has offered become meaningful only when they are considered in relation to the framework within which they occur. Crane mentions three major assumptions. Firstly, Aristotle thinks that "the primary concern of poetics will not be with the actual process of poetic creation but rather with the poetic reasoning — from the character of the end to be achieved to the necessary or desirable means — that is reflected in this process when it terminates in an artistically successful product" (Crane, *Languages of Criticism,* 46). For, the actual poetic process may vary from artist to artist but poetic reasoning or the conception of the type of poetry artists are engaged to compose is more or less the same. In other words, the structural parts of a particular type of work will more or less be the same even when the artists may differ in respect of the particular process they follow to arrange and employ those parts. Secondly, poetics will deal with necessities of two kinds : those which form the essential conditions or parts of all poems and those others which are specific to different poetic forms. What follows from this is that poetics must present a causal analysis of the various poetic species which differ from one another in order to show the necessities which are peculiar to each of the various poetic species. Thirdly, the end of all inquiries of poetics, since it is treated as a practical science "must be the discovery of what is the best possible state, consistent with their specific nature, to which different kinds of poems and their parts may be brought" (Crane, *Languages of Criticism,* 47). These three major assumptions, it is needless to repeat, give Aristotle the basic framework or language of his inquiry.

Crane has also given a list of concepts, methods and approaches derived from aristotle's observation in the *Poetics*, showing how they help us to solve satisfactorily some of our problems in practical criticism. The first thing that we can have from Aristotle is his concept of poetic works as 'concrete wholes'. A concrete whole, as Crane understands, is something the unity of which can be clearly and adequately stated in terms of the particular 'form' and 'matter' it employs. The two aspects, 'form' and 'matter', must join in such a whole, but the form is more important because it is the principle or the cause that gives a definite shape to the 'matter'. Crane illustrates the point with the help of an example. A lump of clay, he says, which is the 'matter' may be given different shapes according to the creator's notion of different particular forms. Matter is thus, in Crane's view, dependent on form for a definite shape. Naturally, in order to understand how form and matter are related in a poem, one must first take into account the formal nature of that poem.

The second important thing, according to Crane, is Aristotle's method of investigation and reasoning. The concept of literary works as concrete wholes gives us a notion about the basic structural relations in a poem. Aristotle framed his method of investigation and reasoning with that notion in mind. The very concept of literary works as concrete wholes organized by formal principles suggests that the critic's problem is to analyse the various elements and subordinate structures of a particular literary work in the light of the particular organizing form of that work. Aristotle's method, Crane suggests, enables a critic, on the one hand, to realize the different forms that can go with different matters, and on the other, to know the different elements or parts of construction that are essentiai for giving a body to some particular form.

A few other terms and concepts may also help us. But Crane Clearly warns — and this is highly significant to indicate Crane's undogmatic stand as a critical theorist — that we must not be statisfied with what we can extract from Aristotle, because the observations of Aristotle — what we get from him in the form of methods and conceptions — cannot satisfactorily explain all the different structural problems which modern works contain. Aristotle considered only that variety of poetry which is imitation, but there are the great varieties of non-imitative species of poetry about which Aristotle said nothing. Even if we talk about the imitative form of poetry we find that Aristotle deals elaborately with only one plot-form which he calls tragic. But there are many other plot-forms which we may and do come across in novels and modern plays about which Aristotle had no scope to talk about. Crane's suggestion, therefore, is that a fresh attempt is necessary for a theoretical analysis, in Aristotelian method, of all the different varieties of structures we meet at present. This implies another important thing which is that poetics is an on-going process. It is not something fixed and determined. New kinds of literature will call for new poetics, or an enlargement of the existing one in order to illustrate the functioning of the new literary works.

Crane may thus be seen to share some of the major theoretical concepts with Aristotle. In his own theory of structural analysis Crane has quite categorically shown what the critic, whose 'intention is to explore the shaping principles of poetic works, is required to do. The critic need not have a thorough knowledge of the variant apparently inconsistent theories of poetry; he need not care for the difference of poetry from other verbal discourses; he need not even worry much about the end of poetry. But the important assumption which the critic must possess is that "any poetic work, like any other production of human art, has, or rather is, a definite structure of some kind which is determined immediately by its writer's intuition of a form to be achieved in its materials by the right use of his medium" (Crane, *Languages of Criticism,* 165). He will, therefore, try to understand what this form actually is, and his knowledge or understanding will be used as a principle in the analysis of that work.

Crane believes that a poem with all its material objects like words, images, symbols, characters and devices of representation is the outcome or effect, the cause of which is the artist's intuition of a particular form that determines the way in which a particular poem appeals to us. In other words, the material objects of a poem are given the power by the poet's intuition of its form to combine themselves and thus affect our ideas and emotions in a particular way. They might easily receive a different type of combination and might appeal to us differently had the form, which is the synthesizing principle, been of a different kind. Hence, the structural problem of a critic is to explain how the material aspects of a particular poem are related to its formal nature. This, however, by no way means that Crane suggests an investigation into the poet's mind to realize his intuition of form. He has warned us against such an assumption by suggesting time and again that the problem of the critic is not psychological but artistic. The poem as a concrete whole is there before the critic, and he must determine the formal nature of the poem from its material objects. Crane thus agrees with Aristotle and disagrees with most of the modern critics who, unlike Aristotle, have defined poetry in general and for whom poetry exists in the verbal universe.

In the field of practical criticism also Crane may be found to follow Aristotelian canons for an effective analysis of the literary texts. In his article "Earnest Hemingway : *The Killers*" Crane proceeds to examine "The Killers" in terms of Aristotelian notion of plot. This is quite justified because "The Killers", though a short story, is full of dramatic elements. The entire story is constituted of a string of conversations connected by a very thin ribbon of commentary. Besides, the story is dominated by action, ending with a definite suggestion of Ole's imminent death. Crane here concentrates his attention on the "technical question of how the characters, actions, and speeches of the boys in the lunch room are related to the situation involving the Killers and Ole Andreson" (Crane : "Earnest Hemingway : *The Killers*", 303). With regard to this consideration Crane divides the characters of "The Killers" into two groups — one belonging to the 'subject' of the story and the other to the 'treatment'. His distinction between 'subject' and 'treatment', Crane admits, is in the sense of what Henry James in his preface to *The Portrait of a Lady* says about that distinction. The subject proper of "The Killers" is comprised of just three characters — Ole Andreson and the two killers, Al and Max. All the remaining characters, according to Crane, are related to the subject only indirectly. They belong intimately to the 'treatment' because they are used as "devices of disclosure and commentary which enable Hemingway to bring his essential 'subject' before us with a maximum of concentration and dramatic liveliness and a minimum of ambiguity as to its desired emotional effect" (Crane : "Earnest Hemingway : *The Killers*", 304). Crane has proved this point with sufficient examples and illustrations from the text. Crane's analysis of the story shows his remarkable ability to handle short story, a genre not known to Aristotle, in Aristotelian terms. The essay seems to suggest that any creative, cognitive discourse is amenable to analysis by Aristotelian criteria. The study is highly original, very profound, and full of critical insights.

In the essay on "The Short Happy Life of Francis Macomber" also Crane applies the Aristotelian canons in order to ascertain the nature of Macomber's tragedy. In order to do this he discusses in detail the essential nature of all Aristotelian tragedy arising out of (i) the formal cause, (ii) the material cause, and (iii) the efficient cause. In the process he also takes up the Aristotelian notion of Catharsis. Crane makes a fine anatomy of the story in great detail and depth, and shows how the story falls to fulfil the Aristotelian criteria of tragedy. Crane, however, does not impose anything on the story from outside (*ab extra*), but elicits the information from inside (*ab intra*) to show how the plot is developed. A true Aristotelian he starts with an analysis of the (desired) effect on the readers and retrospectively identifies the factors that contribute to this effect.

WORKS CITED

1. Aristotle, *On The Art of Poetry*, Trans. Ingram Bywater, Delhi : Oxford University Press, 1985.
2. Crane, R.S., "*Preface*", *Critics and Criticism*. Chicago : The University of Chicago Press, 1957.
3. ——, *The Languages of Criticism and The Structure of Poetry*. Toronto : The University of Toronto Press, 1953.
4. ——, "Earnest Hemingway : *The Killers*", *The Idea of the Humanities and Other Essays, Critical and Historical*, — Vol. II, Chicago : The University of Chicago Press, 1967.

5. Crane, R.S., "Earnest Hemingway : *The Short Happy Life of Francis Macomber*", *The Idea of the Humanities and Other Essays, Critical and Historical*, Vol. II, Chicago : The University of Chicago Press, 1967.
6. Hemingway, Earnest, *The First Forty Nine Stories*. London : Jonathan Cape, 1939.
7. Pritchard, J.P., *Criticism in America*. Ludhiana : Lyall Book Depot, 1970.
8. Vives, Ellseo, "The New Aristotelians of Chicago", *Swanee Review*, Vol. 61, 1953.

8

R.S. Crane and the Theory of Structural Analysis

—Asit Biswas

R.S. CRANE, the leader of the Chicago School of Critics, exerted "a strong and continuing influence on modern criticism" [Fowler 29] after the publication of *Critics and Criticism* and *The Languages of Criticism and the Structure of Poetry*. These books, especially the second one, illustrates Crane's theory of criticism — a theory which was primarily aimed at rectifying the shortcomings of New Criticism as well as placing literary criticism on a much broader and more humane perspective. Crane studies literature as an integral part of a larger problem of human education and considers criticism as essentially a branch of philosophy. For every kind of criticism, he thinks, there is a philosophical foundation to draw sustenance from, and the number of critical positions is, therefore, determined by the number of possible philosophical positions. This belief makes Crane aware of an existence of the multiplicity of critical languages or frameworks, and in order to have best results out of this situation Crane proposes a pluralistic approach to literary texts. His theory of structural analysis, as I will show, has a scope for such an approach. The particular subject with reference to which he elaborates his theory is the structure of poetry. However, Crane uses the word poetry in this context more or less in the Aristotelian sense to mean any artistic creation in words.

I

Before considering Crane's actual theory of literary criticism it will be relevant and fruitful to have a look at the major theoretical concepts on which Crane's critical theory is based. There are critics, Crane observes, like Aristotle who believe in a multiplicity of poetic structures. Side by side there are others like Cleanth Brooks who are of the opinion that the essential structure of poetry is one. Thus they form two different groups of critics having two essentially different attitudes to the problem of poetic structure. Again critics of any of these two groups widely vary among themselves in respect of their individual theorizing. Each critic seems to differ from others in respect of what he says about the structure of an individual poem, no matter whether he believes in the multiplicity or singleness of structure. The reasons behind such wide disagreements can be found in an analysis of critical propositions framed by various critics.

The character of a critical proposition should be determined by three independently variable factors. One factor is the critic himself as a man equipped with certain range of information, intellectual capacity, and a certain kind of taste and sensibility. Another factor is the concrete literary object or the text upon which he is engaged. And a third factor is the power and limitation of the discourse which the critic constructs. Every critic uses a particular framework of selected terms and distinctions and of rules for operating with them with a view to interpreting the text in band. This 'framework' or a particular type of critical language gives sense to a critic's observations. The differences in critical propositions are largely due to the differences of frameworks.

Generally, critical problems are solved and principles derived by means of two different and contrasting methods. In the first method, which Crane calls 'the matter of fact criticism', the critic seeks to present an account of empirically distinguishable literary phenomena in terms of their essential and distinctive causes of production. For instance, a tragedy in this method is taken as a particular type of artistic production having as its distinctive features a particular plot form, character treatment and such other aspects devised in a manner to arouse a specific response. In the other method some abstract principles are at first framed and then applied to the subject in question. Crane calls it abstract criticism. Tragedy in this method may be taken "as the name of a universal attitude or 'vision' of life, the distinctive nature of which is defined in a dialectical opposition to another similarly universal attitude or vision of life for which the word 'comedy' is thought to be the appropriate symbol" (Crane, *Languages of Crilicism,* 2). Critics generally follow either of these two methods. And the important point is that the nature of propositions may and does vary as the one or the other method is taken up. It proves what Crane finds that "literary criticism is not and never has been a single discipline to which successive writers have made partial and never wholly satisfactory contributions but rather a collection of distinct and more or less incommensurable 'frameworks' or 'languages', within any one of which a question like that of poetic structure necessarily takes on a different meaning and receives a different kind of answer from the meaning it has and the kind of answer it is properly given in any of the rival critical languages in which it is discussed" (Crane, *Languages of Criticism* 13).

In such a situation of the multiplicity of critical frameworks Crane intends to offer us the most fruitful method of critical interpretation. And he proposes the theory of critical pluralism which, however, is different from what either S.E. Hyman or R.P. Blackmur suggests. S.E. Hyman and a few other critics yearn for a 'synthesis' of various critical doctrines. The job of an ideal critic, he thinks, should be to combine in his work the best insights and techniques of the large variety of critics. And Blackmur's suggestion is that the only possible way to remove the narrowness of contemporary criticism is to make possible an 'alliance' between different sorts of critics, say, Aristotle and Coleridge. He tells us to collect the important aspects from both Aristotle and Coleridge together. The result, he thinks, will be better than either of the critics taken separately. Both Hyman and

Blackmur fail to realize the actual nature of the problem, and their suggestions, therefore, can hardly solve the problem of varying critical doctrines. What Hyman suggests is merely to make a list of critical insights and techniques. Such a list may only help us giving readymade information about critical solution. And Blackmur's theory of 'alliance' is not a theory at all. It leaves us no scope to identify the virtues of an individual critic.

Crane's theory of critical pluralism is different from the theory of either Hyman or Blackmur. It stands in sharp contrast with the monistic tendency to assert any particular theory as the only correct and profitable one. The pluralistic critic, Crane informs us, "would take the view that the basic principles and methods of any distinguishable mode of criticism are tools of inquiry and interpretation rather than formulations of the 'real' nature of things and that the choice of any special 'language', among the many possible for the study of poetry, is a practical decision to be justified solely in terms of the kind of knowledge the critic wants to attain" (Crane, *Languages of Criticism,* 31). He will be aware of the fact that most of the differences in critical propositions are due to the differences in critical frameworks, and that various critical theories are different but not mutually exclusive. Naturally, even the most diverse sorts of propositions may coexist without any contradiction. A proposition must be judged in terms of the framework in which it occurs. And thus considered, a pluralistic critic will easily get the help of a large number of critical insights, which will enable him to form a more comprehensive approach to literary problems.

To accept most of the critical pronouncements as relevant, however, is by no means to suggest that there will remain no standard for distinguishing the good critical performances from the bad ones. We can, Crane suggests, make comparative valuations among the different existing languages of criticism. We may also judge if a critic, in his act of interpretation, violates the accepted canons of reasoning, hypothesis-making and of common-sense. He must also be true to the literary text he considers.

II

These, then, are the major philosophical assumptions upon which Crane founds his actual theory of critical analysis. But the immediate stimulus behind the formation of Crane's theory of structural analysis came from his dissatisfaction with the critical languages or frameworks of the moderns, specially the New Critics. The modern critics, Crane rightly observes, have defined poetry in general. For them poetry is sometimes 'statement' (as in Winters), or 'communication' (as in Brooks and Warren) or 'knowledge' (as in Prof. Pottle). The moderns thus believe that poetry is a special kind of language used to express thoughts which are impossible to express in other medium. And the business of the critic is to make clear the nature of this language. Their approach may, therefore, broadly be called semantic which, according to Crane, is the latest version of the Hellenistic-Roman subjection of poetics to grammar and rhetoric. The criticism of this sort deals primarily with words and meanings, images and concepts, symbols and referents, with the help of which poets are supposed to constitute the special kind of the language of poetry. And Crane has pointed out — and this is highly original — that although this approach (the semantic approach) seems to enjoy a striking unity of spirit and method, a close study may discover "beneath the common preoccupation of these critics with 'language', 'symbol' and 'meaning', at least two distinctive ways, which are often associated in individual critics, of getting at the semantic nature of poetry and hence of defining the characteristic symbolic structures that condition its meanings and values" (Crane, *Languages of Criticism*, 100). These two different ways within the same approach constitute two distinctive contemporary critical languages.

In the first way, which is followed by such eminent critics as I.A. Richards, William Empson, Wilson Knight, J.C. Ransom, R.P. Blackmur, Allen Tate and Cleanth Brooks, the language of poetry is, generally speaking, considered as statements in words and the initial problem of the critics is to differentiate this language of poetry from other modes of verbal discourse. They proceed, as Crane says, "by fixing upon some familiar type of verbal expression which is admittedly not poetry and then deriving the distinctive attributes and structural patterns of poetry by dialectical comparison and contrast with this" (Crane, *Languages of Criticims*, 100). The critics, thus, preoccupy themselves primarily with the negative analogies between the verbal aspects of poetry and those of science or prose. And so far as the unity and structure of poetry are concerned these critics try to find out the dominant 'attitude' to which all the other thematic elements of a particular poem appear to conform.

The structure of poetry in this approach may be examined in two different but complementary ways. In one way critics may concentrate on the particular manner or technique used in poetry, as distinct from other modes, to apprehend and express meanings. In it, thus, the critic's primary concern will be with the various elements of poetry like rhythm, diction, imagery, symbols, and such others which cooperate in a particular fashion in each individual poem to express and to give force to what the poet tries to say in the poem. In one sense this type of criticism may almost be similar to the formal criticism. But the essential difference is that the elements of poetry in this criticism, unlike those in formal criticism, are treated not as structural parts but as carriers of meanings. Brooks and Warren, Crane has rightly observed, in *Understanding Poetry* have made this method sufficiently familiar to us.

Another way complementary to the first one is to concentrate on the meanings of the poems themselves, not, as it is in the other way, on the technique or manner of meaningful expressions. The critics, Crane observes, reduce the concrete elements of symbols, images, diction and rhythm to some underlying themes or meanings which those elements are considered to embody. A number of New Critics of Shakespeare like Wilson Knight, Harold Goddard, Robert Heilman, and Brooks and Warren in some of their later writings have followed this way of interpretation. In his *The Well Wrought Urn* (27-46), for example, Brooks finds the inner symbolism of *Macbeth* in the recurrent images which relate on the one hand to the clothes and on the other to young and innocent children. Brooks, Crane thinks, has "generalized from them a pervasive opposition between 'the over-brittle rationalism on which Macbeth founds his career' and the 'irrational' forces in life which Macbeth and Lady Macbeth have left out of account in their conspiracy to capture 'the future' for themselves" (Crane, *Languages to Criticism,* 120). My point is that Brooks derives the symbolic structure of *Macbeth* from a consideration mainly of the elements of imagery and diction.

The second of the two contemporary approaches to criticism is popularly called archetypal criticism, and it finds its expression in the works of critics like Maud Bodkin, Kenneth Burke, Edmund Wilson, Lionel Trilling and Northrop Frye. Critics in this approach try to interpret poetry in terms of something else which is considered to be basic in human experience and nature. This other something is either psychology or anthropology, or a combination of both in varying proportions. Actually this approach is based on the achievements in the fields of two non-literary disciplines — the cultural anthropology of Sir James Frazer, Jane Harrison, Emile Durkheim and others, and the analytical psychology of Sigmund Freud and C.G. Jung. These movements had a great influence on this group of critics, poetry for whom is a sort of symbolic language which has close affinities both of nature and of origin with dreams and other psychic manifestations as well as with folk tales and rituals. The starting point of criticism in this approach is not the nature of poetry, but the nature of the universal symbolic process. Consequently, the critical language of this group consists of terms mainly psychological and anthropological.

The structure of poetry to the archetypal critics is more or less identical with the structure of a dream, having at least two levels. And what a critic of this group actually does to expose the structure of an individual poem is, at the first level, to discover the particular archetype which is there in the poem. Mr. Colin Still thus, Crane observes, finds *The Tempest* to have "the double theme of purgation from sin and of rebirth and upward spiritual movement after sorrow and death" (Crane, *Languages of Criticism*, 132). Still discovers the 'rebirth archetype' in *The Tempest* which, he thinks, gives the basic meaning and structure to the work. At the second level the critic draws an analogy between the archetype discovered in a particular work and the work itself in order to convince the readers that the structure and meaning of the work bear similarities to those of the archetype.

Crane considers both symbolic structure and archetypal pattern — the two major critical frameworks of contemporary criticism — inadequate. In order to determine the adequacy of a procedure in practical criticism, he observes, we must take into account the concepts and modes of reasoning which that particular procedure presupposes. We must also see if that procedure can effectively examine all the important aspects of the literary object it takes into its consideration. If any important aspect is left out of account we may suspect the adequacy of that procedure. Crane's impression is that the two contemporary critical languages, when their adequacy is judged in this scale, are proved to be inadequate, because they do not provide us with any "means for dealing precisely and particularly with...the forming principle or immediate shaping cause of structure in individual poems" (Crane, *Languages of Criticism*, 140).

What Crane suggests by 'the forming principle' or 'immediate shaping cause' is that there always remains in the artist's mind an 'intuition of a form' which directs him in what he does with the materials of a work. This 'intuition of form', however, is not thinking, or planning, or incubation, or anything an artist does at the preparatory stage of his writing. From his own experience as an essayist Crane has mentioned that sometimes even after a long and interested concentration on a subject and after collecting all the exciting ideas and patterns of key terms he had to face a lot of troubles to write down even the very first sentence of his essay, whereas, at some other times, he happened to write a whole essay without any trouble or occasional interval even when he was not completely prepared to compose that. What Crane means to suggest here is that there remains something beyond the conscious efforts of an artist which controls his immediate act of construction. This 'something' is, according to Crane, an idea about the particular form which the completed literary work will finally take. The form remains there in the mind of the artist directing him, even though he may hardly be conscious of it, in the act of his actual construction of the artistic whole. This impression of Crane, I think, may help us to understand his stand as a formalist critic. As a formalist Crane gives primacy to form (in this precise sense) over content. He thinks that an artist, even when the content (theme or other materials) is ready in his hand, can hardly construct a successful poetic or artistic whole out of his materials unless the intuition of form is there in his mind as the immediate shaping cause.

The word 'form' is thus used by Crane in a constructive sense, and he considers that 'form' is an indispensable first principle for every writer. So in practical criticism also this may and should be taken as the first principle of the critic. But the two modern approaches to literary works, mentioned earlier, fail to do this for two reasons. The first one is that their critical languages or frameworks lack appropriate terms required to explain the 'formal principles' of the artists. And the second important reason is that these critics in their concern for structure in practical criticism start with some predetermined ideas of poetic structure. Thus the critic who describes poetry as paradox approaches a poem with the determination of discovering paradox. But no such predetermination, Crane suggests, is possible about the 'formal principle' or 'the shaping cause' of a poem. The critic must discover the formal principle from the particular poem he examines by means of his general concepts, And unless and until he discovers the formal principle that enables an artist to synthesize his materials into an artistic whole, the critic can hardly achieve success in analysing the structure, which is the outcome of that formal principle. The languages of the moderns allow to deal only with the various aspects of poetic structure, not with the causes.

III

Now, when some of Crane's major theoretical concepts have been discussed, I may illustrate his theory of structural analysis. He has quite categorically shown what the critic, whose intention is to explore the shaping principles of poetic works, is required to do. The critic need not have a thorough knowledge of the variant apparently inconsistent theories of poetry. He need not care for the difference of poetry from other verbal discourses. He need not even worry much about the end of poetry. But the important assumption which the critic must possess is that "any poetic work, like any other production of human art, has, or rather is, a definite structure of some kind which is determined immediately by its writer's intuition of a form to be achieved in its materials by the the right use of his medium" (Crane, *Languages of Criticism,* 165). He will, therefore, try to understand what this form actually is, and his knowledge or understanding will be used as a principle in the analysis of that work.

Crane believes that a poem with all its material objects like words, images, symbols, characters and devices of representation is the outcome or effect, the cause of which is the artist's intuition of a particular form that determines the way in which a particular poem appeals to us. In other words, the material objects of a poem are given the power by the poet's intuition of its form to combine themselves and thus affect our ideas and emotions in a particular way. They might easily receive a different type of combination and might appeal to us differently had the form, which is the synthesizing principle, been of a different kind. Hence, the structural problem of a critic is to explain how the material aspects of a particular poem are related to its formal nature. This, however, by no way means that Crane suggests an investigation into the poet's mind to realize his intuition of form. He has warned us against such an assumption by suggesting time and again that the problem of the critic is not psychological but artistic. The poem as a concrete whole is there before the critic, and he must determine the formal nature of the poem from its material objects through hypotheses.

Hypothesis-making takes a very significant place, in fact, in Crane's method, and he considers it to be the first important step of the critic's work. The hypotheses, Crane suggests, must not be general but particular, concerned specially with the shaping principles of poetry. And in order to frame his hypotheses a critic must have some theoretical conception about the formal natures and material objects of poetry, although the fact remains that his previous conceptions of forms may be of no use for the poem in hand. Actually, the critic's theoretical knowledge will enable him to form some other hypotheses in the same manner. That is why Crane has suggested the necessity of theoretical analysis, in Aristotelian manner, of those literary genres which Aristotle could not do.

The hypotheses, again, must not merely be descriptive formulae. They must be formed in such a way that they clearly imply practical artistic consequences. Besides, a critic in his act of hypothesis-making must honour every aspect of the text as significant evidence. His hypothesis can never be accepted if it does not suit all the major and minor aspects of the poem. Crane has suggested a method of multiple hypotheses. His point is that the critic will at first frame all the possible hypotheses. In the next stage he will argue against each of them and thus try to dismiss each. In this way one hypothesis will remain, which cannot be dismissed. That will be the most appropriate hypothesis and will illustrate almost correctly the formal cause of the poem in question. A last point Crane mentions is that the critic must try to be as objective as possible at every step of his work.

Crane, however, is quite aware of the fact that all methods have certain defects or, as he calls them, 'characteristic corruptions', and, naturally, the formal approach to the structure of poetry which he speaks of is not free from its defects. Crane himself has mentioned three such possible faults which an incompetent practitioner of this method may indulge himself to make. Firstly, a critic may become merely formalistic in his concern with forms. He may then indulge more in the comparatively mechanical and dry job of analysing the various structural parts and the mechanism of how they combine than in pointing out what gives life to poetry. Secondly, in his concern with poetic wholes a critic may forget the importance of the words in poetry, which actually give a concrete body to a poem. And thirdly, a critic in this approach takes help of theoretical insights to solve the actual problems of structure. His purpose is not to propound or form any particular theory. But the critic may gradually fall into a 'methodological pedantry', and may thus exhibit more interest in pronouncing the theoretical insights relevant to a problem than in the solution of that particular problem.

Crane's awareness of these defects of his own method shows his unbiased outlook as a theorist of poetry. He is among those few theorists who are squeamish about their own theories, and do not claim that theirs are the only faultless and correct methods. However, in spite of its 'characteristic corruptions', the theory of formal inquiry is more applicable to the problems of poetic structure than the contemporary modes of analysis for reasons more than one. Firstly, the faults of the formalistic approach to poetry are not part of the method. They are largely due to a lack of the critic's awareness of his actual work, or to some misconceptions on the critic's part. Naturally, a competent critic may easily avoid them and then give us adequate insights into the structural principles and characteristics of poetic works. Secondly, this method can do all the things which other contemporary modes of criticism usually perform. In an analysis of poetic structures the existing contemporary modes usually confine their investigation to the 'matter' (not 'form') of poetry and to the various techniques in which the matter is expressed in poetry. A critic who follows Crane's method of formal inquiry can and does perform such an investigation into the material elements of the poetry. He may, for example, analyse how various elements in a poem are combined and how they work to create the desired effect; he may also explain the images, symbols, poetic diction and rhythm exploited in a poem, and may even tell us what an archetypal critic informs about the cultural and psychological universals that a poem implies. Thirdly, this approach can perform more than what other modes can, and herein lies the superiority of this mode. Unlike all other modes, the formalistic approach to poetic structure tries to find out the shaping principle of form that makes a poem an artistic whole of a particular kind. All other critical schools, Crane has rightly marked, have been in varying degrees generalizing and reductive. They approach a poem with some definite concepts about poetic structures and try to fit them to poems on the basis of some apparent analogies on the level of the material aspects of the poems. Thus, they reduce structures to a set of concepts.

Such positive values of Crane's theory may convince us of its relative greatness as well as of the liberal mindedness of the theorist. It may still appear to someone that Crane, even when he speaks repeatedly against dogmatism and reductionism, finally propounds his own theory in supersession of all other theories. L.C. Knights, for example, in his review of Crane's *The Languages of Criticism and the Structure of Poetry* remarks : "...having discarded all terms derived from a world of discourse outside poetry Mr. Crane seems to be left with a most meagre vocabulary of appraisal" (Knights 437). Such adverse criticism, however, can easily be disarmed and Crane's Critical stand, which is popularly known as pluralism, may be understood if we follow what Crane has repeatedly said.

The first thing he says is that his theory is "only one of many possible legitimate approaches to the question of poetic structure" (Crane, *Languages of Criticism,* 191). Thus Crane, unlike most other theorists, does not claim that his is the only fruitful and right method. The second important thing is that Crane's theory should not be misunderstood as one capable of solving all the critical problems. It is, Crane suggests, applicable only to the question of poetic structure and not to many other critical questions with which a critic may profitably concern himself. Crane believes that no single critical language can actually bring out the truth about literature. This belief is there as the basis of Crane's pluralism as well as of his disliking for dogmatism and reductionism. It is out of this belief, again, that he welcomes the existence of a multiplicity of critical languages, all of which together can make possible "a fuller exploration of our subject in its total extent than we could otherwise attain" (Crane, *Languages of Criticism,* 193). It is clear, therefore, that to call Crane merely a formalistic critic or a neo-Aristotelian must be a great mistake. For a fuller understanding and exploration of literary texts he is ready to take help of any theory or approach he finds useful to solve his problem. Crane believes, and quite rightly, that the hope for a glorious future of criticism depends on the perpetuation of this multiplicity as well as on an atmosphere of friendly co-operation among all the critical languages.

WORKS CITED

1. Blackmur, R.P., *Hudson Review*, Vol. III, Writer, 1951, 491-97.
2. Brooks, Cleanth, *The Well Wrought Urn : Studies in the Structure of Poetry*. New York : Harcourt, Brace and Company, 1947.
3. Brooks, C. and Warren, R.P., *Understanding Poetry*. New York : Holt, Rinehart and Winston, 1960.
4. Crane, R.S., *The Languages of Criticism and the Structure of Poetry.* Toronto : University of Toronto Press, 1953.
5. ——, ed., *Critics and Criticism, Ancient and Modern*. Chicago : The University of Chicago Press, 1952.
6. Fowler, Roger, ed. *A Dictionary of Modern Critical Terms.* London : Routledge and Kegan Paul Ltd., 1987.
7. Hyman, S.E., *The Armed Vision*. New York : Alfred A. Knoff, 1948.
8. Knights, L.C., *Review of English Studies*. Vol. VI, 1955.
9. Pottle, F.A., The *Idiom of Poetry*. Ithaca, 1946.
10. Winters, Yvor, *In Defence of Reason.* Denver : Swallow, 1947.

9

Literature as Knowledge : Tate's Views

—Samiran Majilya

MORE than any other eminent critic in the twentieth century, Allen Tate (1899-1979) sought to understand and define the nature and function of that 'mysterious apprehension of experience into form' which we call 'literature', without making the reader lose his way in the quicksand of metacriticism and metaphysics or laying himself open to the accusation of creating an esoteric enclave for the critic as the purveyor of recondite terminology. Less of a theorist and conceptualist than any of the American New Critics — a group even otherwise known for its eschewing of excessive jargon or new-fangled phraseology — 'he is afraid that the further criticism advances in system and method, the less aware it becomes of immediate occasions for its use' (Pritchard 246).

Appropriately, the one simple and singular rubric for him is 'knowledge', a word that enshrines for him the core and essence of literature. For Tate the concept of literature as knowledge serves as a bulwark against all kinds of utilitarianism, whether it be those of positivism, scientism, pragmatism or even Marxism. Distressed at the upsurge of utilitarianism in literature, and its degradation of literature to a means rather than an end, a *via media* rather than the consummation devoutly to be wished for, Tate reacted furiously and, in the ultimate analysis, judiciously. While scientism denigrates literature due to its view that the only source of genuine factual knowledge is science, for it alone can yield true knowledge about man and society, logical positivism, as developed by Auguste Comte holds the view that all true knowledge is not only scientific, but must also involve the coexistence and succession of observable phenomenon. This positivism led to its inevitable sequel, pragmatism, an American version developed by William James and John Dewey which justifies everything in terms of their practical effects or contents. 'A catholic and far-sighted theory of the adjustment of the conflicting factors of life is philosophy' (Dewey 5), declared John Dewey, and it is obvious that he expected the same of literature. This kind of scientism, positivism and pragmatism led to the development of I.A. Richards's theory :

> The much more subtle and elaborate impulses which a poem excites are not different in principle. When they have adjusted themselves to one another and become organized into a coherent whole, the needs concerned may be satisfied. In a fully developed man a state of readiness for action will take the place of action when the full appropriate situation for action is not present (Richards 28-29).

Tate notes that the while making such a statement, Richards has added the language of modern psychology to his pragmatism, the language of 'impulse', 'response' and 'stimulus'. The only question such positivists and pragmatists seem to ask is as to whether the poetic response is relevant to the real world and whether it is relevant to action. Tate notes with dismay that 'Poetry has come under the general idea of "operational validity" '(SE 97). He also records with approval Ransom's remarks to the effect that Richards never shows how the ordering effect upon the human mind takes place, and that the entire idea of the coherent whole into which the impulses are organized has no experimental basis, and therefore invalid even in terms of impulses. He sums up the entire literary philosophy of Richards as consisting of three elements : (1) poetry is made of pseudo-statements without referents or actual objects precisely referred to, (2) poetry as an orderer of readers' minds, ordering the mind mysteriously in fictions irrelevant to the actual world, and finally, (3) poetry as a response, a behaviorist readiness for action. For

Tate, poetry is concerned neither with statements nor with pseudo-statements, neither with ordering nor with disordering and finally, neither with action nor with inaction. It is not concerned with any kind of utility, whether material, moral or psychological whether adumbrated by Morris, Winters or Richards. It is noteworthy that T.S. Eliot, similarly anti-pathetic to the utilitarians, refrained from launching a fuller assault only because of his awareness that Tate had already accomplished the devastation of the empirical, logical, positivist and pragmatic attitude :

> ...this trick of making literature do the work of philosophy, ethics, theology, tends to vitiate one's judgement and sensibility in literature, but this aspect has been so well exposed in an essay by Mr. Allen Tate that I shall not linger over it here' (STH 486-87).

Marxist criticism is a special anathema to Tate for he invariably equates such criticism with 'socio-cultural engineering', the habit of using literature as a means of improving society or ameliorating the condition of the proletariat. Tate considers the occasional Marxist rejection of certain kinds of literature to be 'a perversion of the original Platonic rejection of poetry which holds that the arts of sensible imitation are a menace to the political order' (SE 18). Though Tate tars all Marxist criticism with the same brush by failing to note that such crude conceptualization including the determinist view that the basic economic structure (or *base*) engenders a social structure which in its turn generates the literary structure is a 'vulgar Marxism' which is deviant rather than regular[1], his grouse is only nominally against Marxism, his animosity being directed against a utilitarian or deterministic attitude rather than Marxism *per se*. Indeed, referring to Shelley's celebrated dictum that 'the poets are the unacknowledged legislators of the world', Tate declares that the statement is relevant only for 'the true perception that there is always a reciprocal relation between life and art, at the point at which life imitates art' (SE 18).

Since Tate does not reveal any inclination towards any functional attribute of art, whether sociological or theological, affective or psychological, dogmatic or pragmatic, it would perhaps not be inappropriate to ask as to whether he leans towards the opposite extreme of *l'art pour l'art*. Some of Tate's observations do indeed seem to be in defence of this theory, though a more careful observer would notice that such utterances are almost always followed by qualifying statements. Even when he says that 'there is probably nothing wrong with art for art's sake if we take the phrase seriously', he hastens to add, 'and not take it to mean the kind of poetry written in England forty years ago' (SE 595). For him literature 'may be useful', the true art for art's sake viewpoint being acceptable for people who find in art 'things that they can respect apart from use'. Extreme aestheticism, 'a belief in the autonomy of poetry', the belief that poetry is superior to life, is never really accepted by Tate. The ivory-tower 'panaestheticism' of Oscar Wilde which posited that art embraces all life, that art is the standard of life, that life is to be lived for the sake of art — so brilliantly articulated by Wilde in his statement 'I treated art as the supreme reality and life as a mere model of fiction' in *de Profundis*, his accusatory letter to Lord Alfred Douglas — is dismissed as a 'delusion' (SE 19). Alluding to Mallarmé's celebrated belief that poetry is written with words, not with ideas, Tate points out that even if they do not convey ideas, they do convey emotion : 'Poetry, even that of Mallarmé, has some effect upon conduct, insofar as it affects our emotion' (SE 27). He feels that poetry neither tells man what his experience ought to be nor what he ought to do in a crisis, for its only concern is to give man 'the reality of experience'. Surprisingly, in spite of his intense criticism of Yvor Winters[2] for his moral bias, Tate himself reveals a penchant for morality : 'All literature has a social or moral religious purpose' (SE 122). This parallels T.S. Eliot's view expressed in a preface :

> On the other hand, poetry certainly has something to do with morals, and with religion, and even with politics, perhaps (TSW x).

Yet Tate is not in favour of obtrusive morality and ranks Flaubert's *Madame Bovary* above the overtly moral *Uncle Tom's*

Cabin, which he castigates for its making the moral purpose the only justification for the book.

What then does Tate seek in a work of art? The answer is unambiguous — knowledge. Treading the Aristotelian *meden agan*, Tate finds out a solution which is equidistant from the art for art's sake stand on the one hand and the positivist stand on the other. He expresses his concern with knowledge in a statement of seminal importance :

> I have been concerned...with the compulsive, almost obsessed, application of an all engrossing principle of pragmatic reduction to a formed realm of our experience, the distinction of which is its complete knowledge, the full body of the experience that it offers us (SE 105).

To him literature is only 'a way of knowing something...a kind of knowledge that we did not possess before', but he adds on a cautionary note that the knowledge is not about a third thing, for 'the poem is its own knower' and in itself represents the fullness of knowledge' (SE 595), and that 'poetry does not explain anything' (RM 109). What he implies is that it does not give the reader an abstract knoweldge[3] about a particular thing, a baggage which he would be able to carry about with him and use when necessary, but rather that the knowledge is specific to that spatio-temporal situation and for those human agents. The conclusion is inescapable that any dislocation in the setting would lead to an alteration of the knowledge, that the knowledge cannot be extrapolated from the given situation. If Keats had postulated a 'negative capability', Tate proffers his own 'negative postulates' such as the absence of any abstract logic (similar to the Keatsian 'consecutive reasoning') and the lack of any practical use. But it is noteworthy that Tate does not consider such 'special, unique and complete knowledge' to be 'an independent form of knowledge, a kind of cognition, equal to the knowledge of the sciences, perhaps superior' (SE 205). Literature alone provides knowledge of the reality : '...the best way...to look at the actual world under our given condition, is to look at it through poetry" (SE 111). As M. Jancovich observes, "In opposition to mere empirical knowledge of existence, it creates a form of knowledge in which both the rational and irrational aspects of human existence are imaged and imagined' (118). The knowledge that poetry offers must be that of the world, of experiential reality. When he discusses his own poem, *Ode to the Confederate Dead* with the finesse of a *doctor subtilis*, he begins with the declaration that one of the ideas in the poem is that of solipsism, a philosophical doctrine which says that we create the world in the act of perceiving it, but adds that he is himself concerned with 'an experience of it' rather than a 'philosophical statement about it' (SE 595). Like Ransom he suggests that the poet should be pre-occupied with 'the body of the world', but like Beardsley also that the poet is concerned with the concrete universal of real experience, with 'the return of the supra-rational and supra-sensible to the common things' (SE 435).

Tate's alignment with the similar concept of Ransom as regards the presentation of this world is its material, rather than abstract, manifestation is incontrovertible, though Ransom does not quite desiderate knowledge to the extent that Tate does. Both are concerned with the qualitative particularity of the world, for as Ransom emphasizes, the world has body, being made of objects that have 'a qualitative density, or value density' (293). Ransom, too, appears to be anti-utilitarian in his repetition of Schopenhauer's declaration, 'Art is knowledge without desire'. Both feel that the poet makes us realize the world, saliescing what we may have known vaguely or abstractly though this knowing is not simple logical knowing, but what a Keatsian critic would call 'feeling it on our pulses', realizing it with the whole of human existence. Therefore it must involve the polarities and the antinomies rather than with exclusives and unitaries. As William J.J. Rooney so pertinently observes, for Tate, literature implies 'the perfect fusion of the extremes' of 'abstract and concrete, idea and experience, explanation and experience, intellect and emotion, reason and instinct, extension and intensity, denotation and connotation' (293).

For Tate, such knowledge cannot be of anything other than that of the world. He therefore denigrates any poetry that, instead of reflecting the world, is auto-referential, as for example 'poems about the meaning of poetry itself' (SE 215). By this count many of the sonnets of Spenser in *Amoretti*, of Shakespeare in his *Sonnets*, and indeed, Herbert's *Jordan II* would cease to be genuine literature. Tate is indeed dismayed by the fact that never before in history were so many poems written, as in the American English of the century, about poetry. He cites the example of Stevens's *Sunday Morning* which is one of the poet's 'many parables of the poet's relation to the modern world', presenting 'the passive and alienated heroine meditating on the interior darkness of the soul, which would be active and humanly committed, but of refined sense perception, which is passive, and which at last can be aware only of its own ultimate extinction' (SE 216). Even Frost's *Birches*, in which the picture of a boy swinging on a birch sapling turns out to be an emblem of the meaning of poetry, is rejected for the same reason.

The knowledge that art provides is of the 'actual world', so that the writer must relate poetry to the actual world. The actual world is something 'outside' us, something 'objective' and 'empirical', it is something which is opposed to the 'subjective' and the 'private'. Yet even the subjective world is to Tate 'the actual world' in a sense, for 'it sufficiently reflects or gathers in or contains all that we can ever know of any other worlds' (SE 119). But Tate's attitude is ironic towards the Platonic concept of literature trying to directly imitate the actual in the sense of *eidos*, the old theory of imitation which 'sets us off on their old historical merry-go-round' (SE 110). He calls this concept of the relation of the actual world and poetry to be 'the bestiary of the animated cartoon that chase each other's tail until all that is left is a whirling vortex' and a 'fenced-in *a priorism* of the merely philosophical approach' (SE 112). He declares that this has never increased his understanding of literature.

Tate believed that knowledge can only be presented in terms of scene and situation, his statements in this regard foreshadowing that of W.C. Booth in *Showing and Telling*. His approving reference to Flaubert who told Maupassant to go to the station and look at the cab drivers until he understood the typical cab driver reveals his concern with the realistic presentation of both. Analysing his own poetry, he declares that his desire is that they should be 'dramatically relevant', that is 'a relevance discovered in terms of the particular occasion, not historically argued or philosophically deduced' (SE 598). If this is achieved then it can be said that a merely felt or abstract quality of life has been raised to the level of experience, that it has been endowed with form, that 'it has become specific, local, dramatic, formal, that is to say, informed' (SE 598).

Tate provides concrete examples of the knowledge provided by novels, the most noteworthy being Dostoevski's *The Idiot* and Flaubert's *Madame Bovary*. Referring to the 'hovering fly' at the end of Dostoevski's *The Idiot,* Tate reiterates that the actual world can be known only by looking at the imagined scene provided by the novel :

Tate provides concrete examples of the knowledge provided by novels, the most noteworthy being Dostoevski's *The Idiot* and Flaubert's *Madame Bovary*. Referring to the 'hovering fly' at the end of Dostoevski's *The Idiot*, Tate reiterates that the actual world can be known only by looking at the imagined scene provided by the novel :

> We may look at the hovering fly; we can to a degree know the actual world. But we shall not know the actual world by looking at it; we know it by looking at the hovering fly (SE 117).

Of course such a presentation — an accumulation of little actualities — must possess not only actuality but also the magnitude found in the novels of Tolstoy, unlike only magnitude in Thackeray and only actuality in Henry James.

The means by which the literary writer achieves this embodiment or reification of knowledge or the process by which he distinguishes the 'mass language' from the 'language of the people' (SE 57) is 'tension'. By 'mass language' Tate implies the language of ordinary communication, while by 'the language of the people' he signifies the language of literature. Tate derived the term 'tension' — which is significantly the only argot he ever devised — by lopping the prefixes off the logical terms *extension* and *intension*. Poetry of extension is the poetry of denotation, the poetry of abstraction or of logical knowledge. Poetry of intension is the poetry of connotation, the poetry of concrete actuality. For Tate 'good poetry is a unity of all the meanings from the furthest extremes of intension and extension' (SE 63), and what he effectively suggests is that the poem is enriched by 'the dissenting ambiguities at the intensive end of the scale' (SE 64). The similarity of the concept of extension and intension with Ransom's concepts of structure and texture, as embodied in Ransom's statement that 'A poem is a logical structure having a local texture' in his essay '*Criticism as Pure Speculation*' (Stauffer, 110) is inescapable, though Tate develops the concepts to a much greater degree and reveals their relationship more clearly. He even provides examples of 'touchstones' of the 'poetry of center : poetry of tension' (SE 68), some of which are listed below :

> Ask me no more whither doth hast
> The Nightingale when May is past;
> For in your sweet dividing throat
> She winters, and keeps warm her note.
>
> O thou Steeled Cognizance whose leap commits
> The agile precincts of the lark's return...
>
> And my poor fool is hanged! No, no, no life!
> Why should a dog, a horse, a rat have life
> And thou no breath at all? Thou' It come no more,
> Never, never, never, never, never!...
>
> Cover her face; mine eyes dazzle; she died young.

Tate's attitude to literature and the qualities that inhere in literature has never been marked by any orthodox or unitary point of view. He is necessarily catholic, eclectic and heterodox in his attitude to literature, and voices his suspicion of critical methodologies in no uncertain terms :

> It has seemed to me that the best criticism at all times has its best function in the ordering of *original insights* and in passing them on through *provisional frames of reference*, to other secondhand. Eliot may still be our best critic because his constant frames of reference are large and loose, the frame of the particular essay being *improvised, tentative and variable*... (SE 170 emphasis added).

Revealing his distaste for any rigid schematization of such insights, Tate observes that the significance of Henry James's *Prefaces* will always be greater than the schematization of their insights in Percy Lubbock's *The Craft of Fiction*. Tate deprecates 'autotelic' criticism, a criticism that exalts itself above literature, a criticism that is tantamount to the picture apologizing to the frame. Reacting against the imputation that New Criticism refers to a unique or monistic attitude, Tate calls the very concept a 'myth' (SE 169), though he does note that the putative New Critics generally display a hostility to the historical method. But even here, the critical liberalness of one who has been marked out as the sworn enemy of the historical and biographical method comes to the fore when he declares that even the historical method is acceptable when it serves as contributory knowledge and no longer devours the literary text. Calling himself a horse of no particular colour since he adheres to no critical shibboleths, he gives a clarion call for pluralistic criticism : 'Any criticism that increases our knowledge of literature and its availability has its place' (SE 172).

NOTES AND REFERENCES

1. Marx explicitly points out that 'the development of the arts can be out of all proportion to the general development of society, hence also to the material foundation' (Marx 110).
2. Even when Winters acknowledges that poetry is a very complex statement, he sticks to his basic contention that art is moral, as is borne out by the following statement : "According to my view, the artistic process is one of moral evaluation of human experience, by means of a

technique which renders possible an evaluation more precise than any other" (464).

3. Eliseo Vivas's observation is worth noting : 'Whatever contribution the sciences may make towards our knowledge of man, it is to the poet, Mr. Tate answers, that we must go for the *complete* truth about man. The scientist may be able to tell us what man does, and what he can to do, but he cannot evaluate man's actions and elucidate the nature of his norms, and a picture of man that leaves out this aspect of his nature is a sadly incomplete and a relatively trivial picture' (271).

WORKS CITED

Eliot, T.S., *Selected Essays*. Faber, 1951. Cited as STH.

——, *The Sacred Wood*. B.I. Publications, 1976. Cited as TSW.

Dewey, John, *Creative Intelligence*. New York, 1917.

Jancovich, Mark, *The Cultural Politics of the New Criticism*. Cambridge, 1993.

Marx, Karl, *Literature and Art*. New York, 1973.

Pritchard, John Paul, *Criticism in America*. Norman, 1956.

Richards, I.A., *Science and Poetry*. London, 1926.

Ransom, J.C., *The New Criticism*. New York, 1943.

Rooney, William J.J. *The Problem of Poetry and Belief in Contemporary Criticism*. Washington, 1949.

Stauffer, Donald A., ed., *The Intent of the Critic*, Chicago, 1941.

Tate, Allen, *Reason in Madness*. New York, 1941. Cited as RIM.

——, *Selected Essays*. Chicago, 1969. Cited as SE.

Vivas, Eliseo, *Creation and Discovery*. New York, 1955.

Winters, Yvor, *The Anatomy of Nonsense*. New York, 1947.

10

F.W. Bateson's Socio-Historical Criticism : A Reading of William Wordsworth's Poetry

—V. Sujatha

SOCIETY plays an important role in shaping literature. Literature, in turn, reflects the social and economic patterns of the society wherein the art is produced. Literature viewed as a social activity, a criticism of life and a mirror of its age. Northrop Frye believes : "Literature is part of a social process; hence that process as a whole forms the genuine context of literature" (19).

Literature is, in fact, influenced by a number of other factors too, such as history, economics, politics, psychology, autobiography and so on and so forth. In interpreting a literary work, any one or more of these influences have to be studied. The sociological critics will be interested in understanding the social milieu in which the work was produced. Historical critics aim at placing a literary text in its historical context.

Leslie Stephen, a pioneer in the sociological interpretation of literature, defined literature, especially poetry, as the product of the age in which it was created. He comments : "The society and the individual are in thorough harmony and that I take it as the condition of really great literature at all times (129).

In the field of literary criticism, the historical point of view first blossomed in the work of the French critic Adolph Hippolyte Taine, in the middle of the nineteenth century. Taine made his famous pronouncement that works of literature were the outcome of three factors : the moment, the race and the milieu. In the twentieth century F.W. Bateson too applied these factors in the analysis of literary texts, especially poetry.

Bateson's theory is that social influences can affect literature. He points out that poetry typifies, embodies and summarizes the society of its time. According to him, poetry involves four factors — the poet, the reader, a common language and a literary tradition. Literature ceases to be possible, if any of these factors is removed. It is only in the poet-reader relationship lies the essence of poetry. He states : "It is that the historical-sociological approach alone provides the critic with a factual structure to which he can attach his perceptions and generalisations" (EP 258).

I intend to take up here Bateson's criticism of the historical and sociological factors in the literary works of William Wordsworth.

Wordsworth is considered a high priest of Nature. His approach to Nature is mystical as well as philosophical. Though Wordsworth is primarily a poet of Nature, he has, in fact, written a number of poems wherein the primary feelings and affections of the human heart are mirrored. He feels that man was a fit subject for poetic composition.

The age of Wordsworth was revolutionary in two aspects — in politics and in literature. In literature, Wordsworth deviated from the accepted norms of producing art set up in the Classical or Augustan Age. In politics, he experienced the historical events in his time — the French Revolution, the American War of Independence, the September massacres, etc. In addition to these, he witnessed human suffering in the society. These influences left a lasting impression on Wordsworth's mind. The relevance of historical-sociological criticism is therefore indispensable to the criticism of Wordsworth's poetry.

At this stage, some of the longer poems of Wordsworth which involve the society, economics, politics and history of his time are studied.

Descriptive Sketches traces a dominant theme-freedom. It is felt that the people of Wordsworth's age didn't need a government which meant that they wanted nothing but freedom. The composition of the poem grew directly out of his experiences of revolutionary France.

He cries :

> ...Once Man entirely free, alone and wild,
> Was bless'd as free- for he was Nature's child. (520-21)

But soon this freedom flew away because of man's evil nature due to which there was not only poverty, disease, pain and grief, but also oppression and slavery.

The poem reflects Wordsworth's troubled state of mind and hence the mood of the poem is sombre. His hopes of a new golden age after the revolution is expressed in the following lines :

> For ye have reached at last the happy shore,
> Where the charm'd worm of pain shall knaw no more.
> (668-69)

The idea that the common people are surviving in an iron age produced in him a stirring of his poetic energy. This was the decisive moment in the moulding of the long poem *Guilt and Sorrow*. This poem was originally produced as *Salisbury Plain* in which Wordsworth narrates the woe and suffering of a sailor and a vagrant woman who were victims of an imperialist war. The sailor in the poem is forced into hard labour due to which he commits a murder. The female vagrant cries :

> My happy father died,
> When threatened war reduced the children's meal;
> (266-67)

The word 'happy' is indicative of the fact that once the people were happy compared to their sufferings then. The vagrant's father had no hope of any relief to come from unjust military power and many of them have died due to disease and poverty; her father bids trust in God to look after his daughter.

Bateson believes that Wordsworth's object in writing the poem was to expose the vices of the penal law and in influence of the calamities of war on the individuals. He feels that the condition of the have-nots is painted in sombre colours. Commenting on the poem, he states : "The poem had been concerned with the fate of individuals crushed under the Juggernaut of modern society; its villain was the whole contemporary social order" (WR 121).

An Evening Walk describes the history of a poet's evening; it unfolds a sequence of impressions, moods, feelings and thoughts. Bateson feels that it includes the moving account of a beggar woman and her two children. Her husband joins the army due to hunger and gets killed in the "American War of Independence". After his death, she too has been forced into crime and gets separated from the children.

According to Bateson, the theme of separation between child and parent, which seems to be concerned with childhood bliss on the one hand and death and desertion on the other, is a repeated theme in Wordsworth's poetry.

The Borderers written around 1795-96, was cast in a gloomy atmosphere. The problems with which Wordsworth was waging against in *Guilt and Sorrow* continue to find expression in this poem too. A reading of the poem shows that it is an intellectual study of politics based on Wordsworth's understanding of the French Revolution.

Wordsworth created abnormal criminal types, namely that the sailor in *Salisbury Plain* and Oswald in *The Borderers*. Bateson regarded Oswald to be an incarnation of his supposition. He supposes a young man who goes out into the world and betrayed into a crime. Bateson argues that a modern reader would like to know who the young man was. His answer was that the young man was Wordsworth himself because the latter's crime was that he abandoned Annette and Oswald's crime was that he has marooned a captain on an islet.

The Ruined Cottage (later titled *The Excursion*) is a series of poems descriptions and episodes expressing the mind of Wordsworth in middle life. The cottage-weaver in the poem, reduced to misery, runs away from home leaving his wife and children.

This poem also considers the impact of the changes brought about in the industries on the humbler and lower classes of society who are ill-treated and prone to health hazards. Wordsworth also describes in vivid colours the picture of children employed in chimneys and cotton-mills. The gas light, the factory bell and shift work seem to call people at night. Wordsworth felt that the sound of the factory bell was harsher than the death bell.

Bateson assumes that the writing of "The Ruined Cottage" is evidence that Wordsworth has acquired the necessary emotional readjustment in a healthy balance of social detachment and commitment.

When Wordsworth was twenty-one years old, he went to France and observed a number of historical events — declaration of war on Austria and Prussia by France, imprisonment of Louis XVI and the September massacres. The effects of many of these incidents are recorded in *The Prelude or Growth of a Poet's Mind*.

Wordsworth's feeling of hope in expecting triumph of a good cause appears in this poem also as in *Descriptive Sketches*. He asserts :

> ...War shall cease,
> Did ye not hear that conquest is abjured?
> Bring garlands, bring forth choicest flowers, to deck
> The tree of Liberty — My heart rebounded;
>
> (Book III)

Expecting that poverty and inequality would be abolished, he supported the early phase of the revolution. However this only brought him disillusionment. In 1793 there was war between England and France. Its outcome brought for Wordsworth.

...a deep
Imagination, thought of woes to come,
And sorrow for mankind, and pain of heart. (X : 304-06)

Besides the war, in the September massacres created by three men — Marat, Danton and Robespierre, 3000 imprisoned Royalist suspects were slaughtered. The lines which express the emotional shock over the slaughter and massacre are :

...lamentable crimes
'Tis true had gone before this hour, the work
Of massacre, in which the senseless sword
Was pray'd to as a judge; (X : 31-34)

Wordsworth also describes in the poem that the tyrants grew ten times stronger, the land was beset with enemies on every side, people became mad and there were blasts as from hell.

Bateson considers Wordsworth to have become an active political revolutionary only because the latter fell a victim of sexual passion. His illicit love-affair with Annette Vallon, a French lady and the consequent emotional disturbance were also recorded, though indirectly, in this poem, in the long tale of Vaudracour and Julia. Later this tale formed a separate poem by itself.

Bateson's conclusion is that a love-affair in which the homes of the lovers are in different countries cannot be a happy one. It could even be disastrous. Bateson's point here is that the laws and customs in France in the age of Wordsworth forbade Wordsworth a penniless English Protestant, to marry Annette Vallon, a French Roman Catholic.

All the long poems analysed so far which dealt with war, politics and human suffering determined Wordsworth's imagination. They also prove how these causes have played a great role in making Wordsworth the poet that he became.

There are also the smaller poems under the "Lyrical Ballads" and the poems grouped together as "Lucy Poems" which offer us a comprehensive view of Wordsworth's men and society.

For want of space and time, only the longer poems have been analysed in their socio-historical contexts.

The argument of Bateson that a good poem should involve concrete social situations like the battle of Hastings or the Execution of Charles I, is well traversed in many of the poems of Wordsworth. Therefore, Bateson has analysed Wordsworth's poetry through the sociological-historical approach. Bateson opines that one would misread, impoverish or falsify the intention and meaning of the poetry of Wordsworth, if one is unaware of the society, history, politics or economics of the age of Wordsworth. A knowledge of the emotional undercurrents of Wordsworth's life and personality are indispensable if the poems are to be read successfully as poems.

Having considered all the factors which had determined his poetry, one could say that Bateson's historical-sociological mode is necessary as well as useful in the criticism of Wordsworth's poetry.

WORKS CITED

Bateson, F.W., *English Poetry : A Critical Introduction*. London : Longman, 1950. Cited as EP.

——, *Wordsworth : A Re-Interpretation*. London : Longman, 1950. Cited as WR.

Frye, Northrop, *The Critical Path*. London : Indiana University Press, 1973.

Stephen, Leslie, *English Literature and Society in the Eighteenth Century*. London : Gerald Duckworth & Co. Ltd., 1965.

Wordsworth, William, *The Poetical Works of William Wordsworth*. Ed. Ernest D. Selincourt. Oxford : Clarendon Press, 1940. All the quotations of Wordsworth's poems are from this edition.

——, *Wordsworth's The Prelude or Growth of a Poet's Mind*. Ed. Ernest D. Selincourt. London : Oxford University Press, 1970. All quotations from *The Prelude* are from this edition of the text of 1805.

11

Winters on Hopkins

—*Bimalendu Kundu*

WINTERS'S final critical essay in the 1940-49 period is his study of Hopkins's Poetry : "The Poetry of Gerard Manley Hopkins". This is a five part essay, which begins with a comparative consideration of three poems by Donne, Bridges, and Hopkins, respectively, Donne's sonnet. "Thou hast made me and shall thy work decay?", "Low Barometer", by Bridges, and Hopkins's, sonnet, "No worst, there is none". This consideration is based upon "...a particular theory of poetry..." (FC 103) as are Winters's critical essays generally. Moreover, it is a theory to which the poems of Donne and Bridges conform, and which they illustrate perfectly, and from which Hopkins's poem deviates sharply, and "...suffers as a result" (FC 103). But the deviations is not crude or ridiculous and Hopkins has a gift for language comparable to that of Bridges and Donne. Therefore, the deviation and its consequences can be examined without great distraction. The theory of poetry to which the poems of Donne and Bridges conform is Winters's fundamental theory, in which the poem is a statement in words : words are primarily conceptual : words are connotative also, and "...may communicate some feeling and remembered sensory impression as well..." (FC 103). Whatever words communicate will be communicated by their conceptual identity. The poem also has a sound element, a rhythm, which has power "...to modulate and define emotion, so that a finer adjustment of emotion to thought may be possible" (FC 104). The rhythm may also intensify the emotion. In its totality, the poem, then, is not merely a rational statement, but at one time communicates rational understanding and the feeling such understanding ought to motivate. Romantic theory in the eighteenth, nineteenth, and twentieth centuries has increasingly tended to suppress the rational element and to isolate as par as possible, and express the emotional. "This tendency make at best for an incomplete poetry and makes at worst for a very confused poetry" (FC 104).

Taking up the poems themselves, winters finds that both Donne and Bridges "...deal with man's unequal struggle with his lower nature..." (FC 106). Both poems deal with a common predicament, one with an impersonal (Bridges) the other with a personal (Donne) experience. Both deal with experience in general terms, Donne with a theological system as a frame of reference, Bridges with none. In their treatments, "...though both poems are generalized, they are precise..." (FC 107). Hopkins's poem, on the hand, is particularized : "...it deals primarily with a particular and personal experience... (FC 107). It so lacks generalization that the nature of the experience is not perceptible with certainty. Hence "...the mind cannot organize itself to share Hopkins's experience with any real feeling of security" (FC 108). There is a deseparate emotion, but its source is not clear; it is not properly motivated. Moreover, winter feels that the meter of the poem emphasizes the difficulty of understanding it, and supports his view by a line by line metrical analysis in some detail, following a scansion of the complete sonnet. He concludes that Hopkins's work

> ...can be described, and without undue trouble as a variant on Standard English meter, a variant both learned and perverse but in which the rhythm is successfully maintained, in which the perversity is equalled by the skill (FC 112).

The rhythm is fascinating in itself, but it does not exist in itself, it exists in the poem and it derives its justification on the strength of its contribution to the *poeisis* of the poem. In contrast, Bridges's quiet statement, in which the power of the truth stated is directly recognizable, the emotional effect of the language is great in that it has the dignity of conviction. Hopkins lacks a powerful generating concept in his poem : "...since he cannot move us by telling us why he himself is moved, he must try to move us by belaboring his emotion" (FC 113).

In the second section of his essay, winters move to a direct and general consideration of Hopkin's metrical theory. This is an analysis of two documents of Hopkins namely : "Rhythm and other Structural Parts of Rhetoric-Verse" (in the *Notebooks and papers of Gerard Manley Hopkins*) and the "Author's Preface" to the poem selected with an introduction by Helen Gardner in *Poems and Prose of Gerard Manley Hopkins* (London, 1953). The first of these "...is merely a general survey of his speculations on the topic..." the second "...an explanation of his actual practice" (FC 113-14). After a summary of Hopkins's explanation of sprung rhythm in the "Author's Preface", Winters proceeds to a discussion of the technique by means of metrical analysis of "The Windhover" and comments that Hopkins' attempt to express violent emotion through violent meter has got out of hand and become merely preposterous. But we feel that winters has missed the remarkable phono-aesthetic achievement of lines he examines. The circling of the windhover is succinctly caught in the second patterns of the lines. Hopkins obviously knew what he was precisely doing. The substance of Winters's argument is that Hopkins's theory of meter is in conflict with the natural sound qualities of the English language. The central objection which winters has to Hopkins's sprung rhythm, particularly in his more difficult constructions is thus that he uses "...a very complex accentual meter in which the accents are for the most part the irresponsible inventions of the author rather than native elements of the language..." (FC 123). When the author adds to such departures from the natural stresses, so-called "hangers" or "outrides", the complexity for the unassisted reader is intensified by the difficulty of determining whether or not these are to have the characteristics of feet in the scansion of the poem. In effect, therefore, the theory of rhythm which Hopkins uses is not only working against the norms of accent as such, but against the traditions of English Verses as well. Winters feels that the basis for metrical experiments such as those of Hopkins is an inadequate control of his structure by the poet. The source of this defect, as he sees it, is the desire of the poet to intensify an emotion which is either not truly or not adequately motivated by the material of the poem itself. Thus Hopkins's structural technique is in conflict with Winters's basic theory of the relationship of motive to emotion and the need for close rational control of the interrelated conceptual, emotional, and verbal elements of which the poem is composed.

In the third section of his study, Winters considers a common method of presenting a landscape followed by an application, usually religious. Winters feels that this method has certain inherent difficulties which he attempts to illustrate by reference to various poems and lines by Hopkins. He considers first the lines of Hopkins's well known sonnet :

The world is charged with the grandeur of God.
It will flame out like shining from shook foil :
It gathers to a greatness, like the ooze of oil
crushed....

Winters observes that the poet begins by presenting an important concept in impressive phrasing. But instead of developing the concept, after the manner of the Renaissance poets, he illustrates it with indeterminate images the inadequacy of which is apparent, whether the lines are regarded grammatically of psychologically. *The Starlight Night* illustrates for Winters a structural difficulty in several Hopkin's poem using the landscape as a source of spiritual signification where the spiritual theme is not fully developed. Winters object to Hopkins's frequent use of this method of using a landscape as a direct motive for a feeling which is too powerful for such a motive "...and then to append the perfunctory moral as a kind of theoretic justification" (FC 126). Among other poems in which this technique is used more or less, are : "Spring", "The sea and the skylark", "The windhover", "Pied beauty", "Hurrahing in Harvest", and "Duns Scotus's Oxford". "Duns

Scotus's Oxford", for example, does not define its subject and support it with perceptual evidence. Rather it presents empty epithets and gives a merely sentimental mention to its subjects.

Since "The windhover" was acclaimed by Hopkins himself his best poem, and is accepted as such by many of his admirer, Winters gives an extended consideration of its thematic structure, developing his own perspective in relation to those of McLuhan, Pick, and Ruggles (See FC 127-35). His method of considering the poem is to question several details of figure or language in the poem. In the octet he finds that there is a fine description. But this much discussed description of the bird in flight "...in itself...is merely description, that is an example of the simplest subject matter available to the poets" (FC 127). He feels that, as description, this one can be equalled or surpassed by many such description in Coleridge, Wordsworth, Keats, and Hardy. He calls particular attention to Hardy's night hawk in the poem, "Afterwards". Hardy not only achieves an excellent description, in which every detail reinforces every other, but he avoids the pathetic fallacy of Hopkins, by which the latter reads his own ecstasy into routine action of the bird. In the *sestet*, in which the thematic explanation is offered, Winters finds difficulty with the meanings of the terms, "buckle", "chevalier", and the meaning of the phrase, "makes plough down sillion shine". Analysing the several interpretations of Pick, McLuhan, and Miss Ruggles he finds them unacceptable generally for philological, linguistic or physical reasons (FC 134). He is inclined to agree with Miss Ruggles's view that the Windhover is Christ and Christ is Windhover. And he finds such a conception as the unifying image of a poem on Christ unacceptable :

> To describe a bird, however beautifully, and to imply that Christ is like him but greater is to do very little toward indicating the greatness of Christ (FC 133).

Winters's view is that the Windhover is an instance in which a poet takes advantage of the Romantic sentimentalism by which birds are viewed as symbols of the free and unrestrained human spirit in the manner of Shelley's "Skylark". This kind of notion is to Winters an example of an attempt to embody a meaning without the meaning being given.

In concluding his remarks about the use of nature as a structural device for the development and communication of spiritual meanings, and in particular his judgment of "The Windhover", he finds that in his poem there is assertion — but no explanation and description — of importance and excitement. Moreover, Hopkins violates grammar at convenience to gain effects which, to him, are more important than grammar — namely striking epithets and phonic effects. But

> ...the phonic effects are frequently over-wrought and badly wrought, and the epithets, when they do not overwhelm the subject with an assortment of ill-adjusted details, are likely to be incomprehensible because of the way in which they have been attained (FC 135).

Winters misses the point that the bird dose become first a metaphor and then a symbol, and the structure of a symbol is always different from the structure of the object symbolized. So it is meaningless to point out that the haecceity of the bird is different from the haecceity of Christ. The difference is only natural. In "The Windhover", the octet presents an impressive, though overrated description of the bird. The bird appears to symbolize the perfection of Christ but the haecceity of the bird and the haecceity of Christ are distinct, and the poem tells us nothing of Christ's haecceity. Unless Christ is symbolized, however, the structure of the poem fails because the Windhover could justify the excited tone. In shore :

> The poem is romantic — both in its over-wrought emotionalism and in its carelessness. It is not the greatest sonnet ever written, nor even the best poem in Hopkins : it is a poem of real, but minor and imperfect virtues, and that is all (FC 135).

It is not really over-wrought, because ecstasy that it tries to describe is, by nature, a state of heightened emotion. The fourth section of Winters's study of Hopkins is an attempt to discover in Hopkins's history the source of the kind of poetry he has written. He considers the psychological crisis of Hopkins's later years as a source of some of the qualities of his verses, specifically of his lack of intelligible mastery of this crisis as it is revealed in the poems "...an element of emotional violence which is neither understood nor controlled" (FC 136). Winters also seeks a possible source of Hopkins's theory and practice in Hopkins's interpretation of catholic doctrine and finds a basis for an answer in an undated fragment entitled "on a piece of Music", and on a discussion of its content by John Pick. Winters refers to Pick's statement that this fragment "...makes the important distinction...between art and prudence" (FC 138). In the somewhat standard explanation of Maritain to which Pick refers, this is the distinction between art, which operates "ad bonum operis", and prudence which operates "ad bonum operantis". Art as such has no other end than the perfection of the work made, and not the perfection of the man making. This is New critical stand. This vital distinction, derived from St. Thomas Aquinas, is markedly different from Winters's own view of the matter.

Winters explains his view, which he differentiates "radically" from those of St. Thomas and Hopkins. The basis of this view is his often repeated view that

> ...the poem is a rational statement about a human experience, made in such a way that the emotion which ought to be motivated by that rational understanding of the experience is communicated simultaneously with the rational understanding : the poem is thus a complete judgment of the experience, a judgment both rational and emotional (FC 139).

To Winters the distinction of the moral value of art from the moral value of prudential action is invalid :

> The poetic medium is simply a means to a finer and more comprehensive act of understanding than we can accomplish without it. The poem thus falls under the heading of prudence, to continue with the scholastic terms; it is a method for perfecting the understanding and moral discrimination; it is not an obscurely isolated end in itself (FC 139).

Winters feels that this is a more Thomistic interpretation on the matter, when it is related to St. Thomas's philosophy "as a whole" than is either Pick's or Maritain's. His reason is that his own theory "...relates a major human activity to the whole of human life, to the economy of redemption, so to speak, and does not leave it dangling" (FC 139). In defending his own view that art is in the "prudential" order, Winters points out that St. Thomas did not treat art systematically as he did other matters, but rather used his limited notions of art to illustrate other matters. So, St. Thomas's ideas of art must be derived from "...many brief and scattered comments..." (FC 139). In searching St. Thomas, Winters finds no clear statement which will support Winters's own view, but he does find statements which make Pick's opinion appear doubtful.

Winters is not primarily concerned with St. Thomas, but he feels that the influence of St. Thomas has been so great that he must point out the limitations of St. Thomas's theory. One of these is that "...he appears to find a common quality in what we call the beauty of nature and in what we call the beauty of art" (FC 140). Here we find the sharp differentiation between art emotion *vs.* life emotion — change of medium — imitation of the universal principle involved in nature. The natural object is outside the moral order, man's apprehension of it and evaluation of it is in the moral order since it can occur only in an act of criticism or a work of art. If the artist is viewed as one who creates outside the moral order then the conception of what he has done will naturally result in some version of the art for art's sake theory. In Winters's view, the natural object cannot be conceived as a work of art because it is not made in consequence of a human judgment; it thus is a possible subject for art, but cannot be art unless it is creatively acted upon by human judgment. Returning to Hopkins, Winters refers to an early composition *On the Origin of Beauty, A Platonic Dialogue*, which is included in *The Notebooks and Papers of Gerard Manley Hopkins*. This, which follows St. Thomas's notion, starts by deriving principles of beauty from a consideration of natural objects, and concludes by discursing beauty entirely in terms of construction. Thus the form becomes "...a thing and an end in itself" (FC 141) and the theory becomes a version of art for art's sake. Citing a letter which Hopkins wrote in 1868, Winters points out that in this instance Hopkins modifies his view to the extent that he admits "...that a work may have an *art value alone*, but that it should also deal with an innocent subject, that is, should not be immoral" (FC 141). Yet even here the two concepts of art and morality are distinct so far as their functional relationship is concerned.

Thus Winters finds in Hopkins, as in St. Thomas, no basis for a clear concept of moral quality in a literary work. The reason for this is that Hopkins, as a student of St. Thomas, accepts the scholastic distinction of the artistic order from the prudential order. Since art operates "ad bonum operis" there is in Hopkins's notion no provision for a moral value in the work of art.

Winters's objection to this is a necessary consequence of his own theory. In his view, the procedure by which a poet structures his subject in a literary form is in the prudential order in so far as the critical intelligence and reasonable control by that intelligence operate to make the poem and moral result of an act of evaluation. The finished work in his view, becomes moral because it represents, in the form which has been given to its subject, evaluative judgments. What Winters is aiming at becomes clear from his stated deduction from Hopkin's theory :

> These ideas will justify (within the limits mentioned) a perfectly romantic art : emotional intensity for its own sake, metrical elaboration for its own sake, repetition and elaboration of structure for their own sakes (FC 142).

Winters says that the poem becomes an unrestrained indulgence in meaningless emotion, and an unrestrained exercise in meaningless ingenuity; the poet has no responsibility to understand and evaluate his subject truly. Hopkins's theory is then a Romantic theory, because in it the poet has no responsibility to understand his subject and evaluate it truly. The results of such a theory can be seen in "The wreck of the Deutschland", "Spelt from Sibyl's Leaves", and "Binsey Poplars", among others of Hopkin's poems. In them, Winters finds a slight paraphrasable content upon which such fantastically elaborate structures are built, that the subjects are all but lost.

Winters feels that W.A.M. Peters's study of Hopkins, Gerard Manley Hopkins : *A Critical Essay toward the Understanding of his Poetry* (London, 1948) again demonstrates an essential "Romanticims" in Hopkins. In dealing with Hopkins's Scotist doctrine, Peters points out that Hopkins was preoccupied with his own "inscape". To Winters, the doctrine of *haecceitas* in Scotus is

> ...merely an attempt to describe in metaphysical terms the observable fact of individuation, and it involves no sentimental preference for the preservation of any given state of individuation (FC 143).

But Hopkins, in Winters view, used his notion of *haecceitas*, as the basis for justifying the expression of his own soul. This, to Winters, is indistinguishable, from Romantic doctrine and he directly opposes it on the basis of his own theory :

> In my terms, it is the business of the poet, not to communicate his own inscape, but to arrive at a true judgment of his subject whatever it may be; we all have individuality, but few of us have intelligence (FC 144).

So, to Winters, Hopkins is a Romantic one who, like Poe, committed himself to bring originality to English poetry. Winters feels that English poetry is the greatest single body of literature produced in Europe since the Greeks. If this great monument lacks originality, then he suggests that perhaps originality is not an essential to greatness. Among Winters's great poet — Donne, Jonson, Herbert, Greville, and Bridges — he finds a minimum of eccentricity, and likeness in tone and method. Moreover, these poets are interested not in exhibiting themselves but in exhibiting truth. To Winters, Hopkins is not interested in exhibiting truth. In Hopkins, rather,

> ...we have a poet who is concerned with the expression

> of his own inscape (Self-expression) and with the inscapes of natural objects and with little else, [thus] we may expect him to produce poems which are badly organized, and loosely emotional, and which endeavor to express emotions obscure in their origins and to express emotions in terms of natural details of landscape to which the emotions are irrelevant. And poems of this kind are what Hopkins most often wrote.... Hopkins is a poet of fragments for the most part, and it is only if one can enjoy a chaos of details afloat in vague emotion that one can approve the greater part of his work (FC 145).

This is not quite true. Most of Hopkins's better known poems are complete in every respect. In "Felix Randal", for example, he explores the man in his distinct individuality and the concluding line, through a sudden flashback, brings the past and the present into a significant relationship that gives substance to a vision.

The final section of the essay is a summary attempt by Winters to indicate his answer to the question, "What then, can we salvage from Hopkins?" Here he is concerned with Hopkins, the artist, and generally restricts himself to structural characteristics rather than to ideology, or poetic theory of Hopkins. That his approach is so restricted is indicated by the fact that the sixteen poems he refers to in this concluding section, are poems he has not dealt with in the earlier section of the study. From these poems, and with a variety of methods of discussion, most of them briefly developed, Winters chooses the following as "the most nearly successful poems" : "The Habit of Perfection", "The Valley of the Elwy", "Inversnaid", "St. Alphonsus Rodriguez", and "To him who ever thought with love of me." Admitting that his survey is short and incomplete, but noting that it..."is the outcome of more than thirty years reading of Hopkins..." (FC 153) he feels that these five poems are the best of Hopkins. Regarding Hopkins's rank as a poet, Winters concludes :

> If one were to name the twelve or fourteen best British poets of the nineteenth century, Hopkins would certainly deserve a place among them, and I think his place will be

> permanent; but the place is not the place of the greatest, nor even of one of greatest (FC 154).

In spite of his occasional crtical myopea on account of his emphasis on reason and distrust of emotion, Winters's judgment of Hopkins is, by and large, biased. But his quarrel with Hopkins's deliberate distortion of language has a point. It is not for nothing that the technical innovations of Hopkins have been studiously discarded by poets like Eliot, Yeats an Larkin, for example.

WORK CITED

Winters, Yvor, "The Poetry of Gerard Manley Hopkins" in *The Function of Criticism : Problems and Exercises.* Denver, Swallow, 1957. Cited as FC.

12

Winters on Yeats

—*Bimalendu Kundu*

IN the eassy "The Poetry of W.B. Yeats", Winters's final critical writing included in *Forms of Discovery* (1967), the approach is characteristic. Winters's initial interest is in Yeats's thought as an ingredient of his verse, and his initial assumption is that the understanding of Yeats's thought is essential for a correct assessment of his work. Citing Unterecker's guide, Winters objects to the unquestioning acceptance of Yeats's ideas regarding the nature of poetry, and the unquestioning acceptance of the greatness of Yeats as a poet as well. Yeats had an occult symbolic system from which many of his poems derive their meaning. Yet the universal harmony which is the upshot of Yeats's scheme of symbols, is confusing when viewed in the light of symbolism itself. The mediaeval symbol "...refers to an object which has a one-to-one relationship to a meaning; that is, the whale is Satan, and Dante's panther, lion and wolf are lust, pride, and avarice" (FD 206). The mediaeval symbol functions more like an allegory — the kind of one-to-one correspondence that we have, for example, in Dante's *The Divine Comedy* — than in a symbol proper. Even in romantic poetry the symbols become complex. Shelley's Skylark or Keats's nightingale are not just universal or algebraic symbols. With Mallarmé and Yeats symbols become more complex so that the meanings of the swans of Mallarmé or Yeats arise from the varied inherent suggestions of the poetic object. It is through intensely personal, private or esoteric symbols that the inner world of consciousness is manifested. The symbol in Yeats, however, is generally the modern type of French symbolist poetry.

But the symbolic system of Yeats, so essential to the understanding of his poetry, is traced by Winters to French symbolist poetry in general, and to Mallarmé, in particular. In this conception of Yeatsian symbol Winters finds an aim "…to produce a kind of poetic absolute in which rational meaning would be as far as possible suppressed and suggestions would be isolated" (FD 206). As he had in "Poetic Styles Old and New", Winters equates this conception of the symbol, what Frank kermode calls the "romantic image",[4] that is, "…the image which is meaningless, inscrutable…" (FD 206). Winters points out that Yeats did not simply compose his poem.

Within the limits of this symbolic system, rather he "…wrote forthright poems; and he often wrote in symbols more nearly akin to mediaeval symbols than to Mallarmean" (FD 207). Moreover, the symbols themselves are means of expressing Yeats's ideas, and the ideas, like the symbols are somewhat personal to Yeats. Winters finds among them a number of arbitrary personal conceptions, some of which clearly conform to the anti-intellectual tendencies of Romanticism. Winters's criticism of Yeats clarifies by negative example his ideal for the use of symbol. Yeats's symbols, Winters says, do not give us real meaning", but only the feeling of meaning — what Winters calls "pseudo-reference" full of the "sickness of ambiguity". The symbols go wrong, Winters states, because the ideas are wrong, and he cites several of Yeats's "wrong" ideas that for him evoke false symbols : All good comes from the emotions; madness is good; wisdom is condemned, ignorance praised : lust and rage are virtues; sexual union and mysticism are equated, or at least, sexual union "…participates in the mystical experience in a literal way" (FD 207). For Winters, the complexity of Yeats's symbols falls short of greatness because they are not motivated "morally" with the proper relationship of content to style, and hence they are unreasonable.

Winters also explains Yeats's sociology. His ideal society is agrarian, with a dominant landed gentry and a peasant class kept in its place. Politicians and tradesmen are kept as few as possible. For picturesqueness this society would have "...a fair sprinkling of beggars (some of them mad), of drunkards, and of priests (FD 207). The gentlemen of this society — violent and better men — should be patrons of the arts and guardians of order. They should be fond of hunting and fishing. The ladies should be beautiful and charming, gracious; they should be musicians if possible, should drive men mad, should love, marry and procreate, should not be intellectual and should ride horses preferably to hounds (FD 208). In short, he wanted an eighteenth century Irish society, far from the "...political and/or argumentative turmoil of revolutionary Ireland" (FD 208). In this regard Winters anticipates Eagleton who contends that "Yeats's consciousness of his social disinheritance is precisely what fuels the process of his poetic maturation, and his poetry turns in the early years of this century from narcotic fantasy to the stripped, toughened forms of a bitter, yet defiant disillusion."

Above all, Yeats had cosmological and psychological systems which are ideological bases for his poems. The central idea in his thinking is a cyclical concept of history, with a two thousand year cycle beginning in objectivity and ending in dispersal and a new beginning. He believes that the human experiences a similar cycle. For his cyclical process, Yeats had two diagrams that of "the phases of the moon" and that of "the interpenetrating cones (gyres, pernes, or spindles)". According to Winters, Yeats's dependence in his early work of the Celtic period on figures of Irish legend, and his later creation of such characters independently were added to these ideas. In his work there are also evidences of his transforming into heroes himself and his friends, such as J.M. Synge, the Grogor's, Maud Gonne, Shawe — Taylor, and Hugh Lane.

Turning to the poems themselves, Winters first considers those related to Yeats's theory of the historical cycle. He analyzes the thematic material of "Leda and the Swan", "Two Songs From a Play" and "The Second Coming". Winters reads "Leda and the Swan" as a depiction, in the rape of Leda by Zeus in the form of a swan, as the end of the first and the introduction of the second cycle of Greek civilization. The "Two Songs From a Play" are a description of "...the end of the second Greek Cycle and the beginning of the Christian" (FD 210). "The Second Coming" prophesies the imminent end of the Christian cycle (FD 210). Winters marks that all of these poems deal with violence, and that Yeats admires violence; thus he negates Platonic tolerance, Doric discipline and Christian Civilization. Although Winters finds some value in the "sonority of these poems, the intricacy of Yeats's private mythology renders them unsuccessful as poems. There is inadequate motivation in the tenor of the poems for the vehicle by which Yeats expresses it. In respect of "The Second Coming" this is a particularly glaring weakness :

> ...if we are to have a poem dealing with the end of civilization and one that we can suppose to be great, the poem must be based on something more convincing than a home made mythology and a loose assortment of untenable social attitudes (FD 214).

Winters considers "Sailing to Byzantium" and "Byzantium" generally unsatisfactory, although frequently satisfying in certain stanzas and lines. He objects particularly to the use of unrealized figures of speech, in which "...the vehicle or the descriptive matter is dead..." (FD 214). In such figures the reader is required to deduce meaning from the illustrative material which has no such meaning. He suggests that the introduction of precise abstract language into "Sailing to Byzantium" would enhance its capacity in meaning — hence its quality as a poem. He suggests also that the writing of the last stanza, which he regards as well written, is weakened by the distressing introduction of a poor portrait of God and the bardic conception of the poet.

Winters finds the meaning of "Byzantium" fairly obvious : Byzantium is eternity. In "Sailing to Byzantium" the poet was dealing with his voyage to eternity; here the poet is looking out from eternity on those who are entering. Although the symbolism in the poem is Yeats's private system, and understandable enough from that system, it does not communicate adequately a meaning beyond the sensory level. It is decoration and fails to clarify the meaning of the poem. The difficulty with this kind of writing is that : "The generality of the meaning…has nothing in common with the precise generalization of abstract terms" (FD 218). Such use of private ornament is attempting to express ideas in terms of sensory details and it fails because "…his sensory details do not embody definite thought…" (FD 218).

Winters's stanza by stanza analysis of "Among school children" uncovers easy allusion, instead of substance, in Yeats's of confused mythography of Helen of Troy and Maud Gonne. There is moreover shoddy diction, careless violent diction, and irresponsible management of the scarecrow symbol. The final stanza is understandable to Winters only

> …in terms of the pseudo-mysticism and anti-intellectualism of the past two hundred and fifty years but which I cannot grasp imaginatively — that is, in terms of human life as I know human life (FD 220).

"Among School Children" is ridiculed for its conclusion "How can we know the dancer from the dance?" "If the dancer and the dance could not be discriminated in fact, the dancer could never have learned the dance" (FD 220). Winters finds some merit in lesser known poems but concludes that "it is impossible to believe that foolishness is greatness". Yeats's self-assertion, the bardic tone, the anti-intellectual drift of his work, its emotional heat, account for his success (FD 234).

According to Winters, a number of Yeats's poems exhibit a habit of over-dramatization. He finds in such works as "A Coat" and "On Those That Hated The Playboy of the Western World" an inflated and bardic style that is weak by comparison to the witty and unpretentious style of Synge when the latter dealt with similar topics. "To a Friend whose Work Has Come to Nothing" is plain and honest and exhibits a certain moral nobility in its first ten lines, but it generally exhibits not only an inflated style, but recommends madness as a cure for the thematic problem. Although "In memory of Major Robert Gregory" has been widely praised, Winters thinks that it is "…a very bad poem".

The work, the twelve stanzas, fails in its awkward language, stereotyped detail, and mechanical devices for achieving over-emphasis. Above all he finds the portrait of Gregory over-blown, and the poem a generally "loose structure" (FD 225). "Coole Park", honouring Lady Gregory and her home, is "...a typical meditation on the virtues of old families and their patronage of the parts, but especially upon Lady Gregory as a force in bringing distinguished men together and guiding their work" (FD 225). Winters feels that the poem is weak in details of figurative language, in sentimentality, in verbiage for the sake of verbiage. "The Municipal Gallery Revisited" is the "...best poem of this kind..." (FD 226) to Winters, although it has marked metrical limitations in its variance from the lambic pentameter norm. Although the last stanza over-values Yeats's friends in the characteristic manner of this group of poems, still it "...is the moving statement of an old man who held them in high esteem and who now reviews their official portraits, all of them being dead" (FD 227). Although he thinks "Easter 1916" the best of Yeats's political poems, Winters finds fault with the refrain. "A terrible beauty is born" as understandable sentiment spoiled by diction which is "pure Yeatsian fustian" (FD 227). The central idea of the poem is that "...truly spiritual life consists of momentary change; fixity of purpose turns one to an imperceptive stone" (FD 228). Winters rejects such a view in that it is simply a familiar Romantic doctrine not to be taken seriously.

The most nearly successful of Yeats's poems, in Winters's view, are "The Wild Swans at Coole", "I am of Ireland" and "Long-legged Fly". "The Wild Swans at Coole" is perhaps the best of these. Winters interprets this poem as a work in which "...Yeats sees in the swans a symbol of his poetic power, still present, but soon, perhaps, to be lost" (FD 230). In these terms he finds the poem both clear and fine. The opening description of the dry autumn at twilight and the brimming water are "...two unobtrusive but brilliant details, the effect of which seems to permeate the entire poem" (FD 228). "I am of Ireland" is concerned with a slight subject, an unwelcomed invitation to the poet to enter Irish politics. Yet "...the movement and diction are masterly" (FD 231). A defect is that the poem lacks information which would make it more fully understandable. "Long-legged Fly", to Winters, is one of the most interesting poems of Yeats. But it does have thematic defects, for example, Yeats's pseudo-religious glorification of sexuality in portraying Michel Angelo's motive for painting Adam in the Pope's Chapel. However, "The descriptive detail is throughout the poem and the movement of the lines are about equally beautiful" (FD 232). Of the minor poems, Winters feels that "For Anne Gregory", "Crazy Jane Grown Old Looks at the Dancers", and "Lullaby" are graceful, though slight. "After Long Silence" and "The Cat and the Moon" have mixed value, the first being somewhat obscure, and warped in its preference for youth, love, and ignorance over wisdom. "The Gyres" though badly written, is revealing of Yeats's cosmology and social doctrines. The six poems grouped in "Under Ben Bulben" also summarize his ideas and attitudes. In the fifth is a succinct summary of his social ideas, and his attitude toward himself is summarized in the sixth.

Winters's conclusions regarding Yeats are related to the central problems of his obscurity, that is, the confusing character of his symbols, his ideas, and his style. He feels that Yeats's symbolism, was not primarily that of Mallarmé. And Winters is primarily right, because although Yeats was influenced by Mallarmé and Mallarmé was influenced by Baudelaire, Yeats's involvement in the Celtic Movement and his interest in the occult forced him to devise his own esoteric symbols. So, in spite of a generic affinity Yeats's symbols remain distinct from the symbols of Mallarmé. Furthermore, from "Responsibilities" onwards he became more and more openly didactic. He tried to persuade his readers of the values of his ideas, but in Winters's view, "...unfortunately his ideas were contemptible" (FD 233). While worthwhile in some of his minor poems and in many fine lines and passages in his major works, still the weakness of his ideas prevents him from being a major poet. Many have regarded him as a great poet and his reputation is easily explained. First of all, he has real talent, evidences of which are scattered through his work. Secondly, contemporary readers who often fail to recognize a relation between motive and emotion or between thought and poetry, overlook his defects in this matter. Winters emphasises the balance. The balance in a poem may be that of idea to feeling, or meaning to feeling, structure to emotion, logical content to emotion, the rational structure to the rhythm, or the meanings to the convention. Thirdly, his "bardic tone", that is, his power of self-assertion overwhelms his readers.

To Winters, "...Yeats was not a great poet, nor was he by a wide margin the best poet of our time" (FD 234). Yet for most of his readers the bardic tone which he affected is synonymous with greatness. Winters feels that the effect of this tone will diminish with time, and that Yeats's reputation will diminish similarly. But in the meantime, he is concerned, that the popularity of Yeats can do a good deal of damage :

> In our time Yeats has been regarded as the great poet in person, the poet of the impeccable style. He has thus become a standard for critics, with the result that the work of better poets has been obscured or minimized; and he has become a model for imitation, with the result that the work of a good many talented poets has been damaged beyond repair (FD 234).

WORKS CITED

Eagleton, Terry, *Criticism and Ideology*, Thetford : The Thetford Press Limited, 1976. Fifth Impression, 1986.

Kermode, Frank, *The Romantic Image*, New York : The Macmillan Company, 1957.

Unterecker, John, *A Reader's Guide to William Butler Yeats*, London : Thames and Hudson, 1959.

Winters, Yvor, "Poetic Styles, Old and New". In *Four Poets on Poetry*. Ed. Don Cameron Allen. John Hopkins University Press, 1959. Cited as FPP.

——, "The Poetry of W.B. Yeats" in *Forms of Discovery*. Denver : Swallow, 1967. Cited as FD.

13

Linguistics and Literary Criticism

—*M.P. Sinha*

LITERARY criticism is a body of principles that define literature and function as guidelines for the analysis and evaluation of a literary text. Because literature is the most comprehensive study of man, it evokes response from all corners. People from different walks of life create, appreciate and evaluate it.

The early critics, Plato and Aristotle, were philosophers who placed literature in their philosophical systems and defined and interpreted literature accordingly. Plato considered it to be twice removed from reality, an imitation of imitation, hence useless whereas Aristotle explained it as creative imitation of reality and, therefore, as real and useful as reality. The mimetic theory continued till the Augustan age and literature was considered a mirror of reality. Coleridge and Wordsworth and the German critics considered it to be a lamp that showed reality. In both cases literature was considered to be at a distance from reality whether it was a mirror or a lamp.

It is in this context, we can understand the impact of linguistics on literary criticism. The Russian Formalists, all famous linguists, rejected the age-old concept of the separation between literature and reality and posited the view that reality is there in the text itself and literature is a semiotic mediation of reality. The basis of this new concept of literature is Ferdinand de Saussure's concept of the arbitrary relationship between the signifier and the signified, the sign and the concept.

The Russian Formalists, French structuralists and post-structuralists have all taken help of modern linguistics which assigns the role of language in society in a much more important way than hitherto thought of. No doubt, critics like Longinus, Dryden, Pope, Dr. Johnson, Wordsworth, Coleridge, Richards, Empson, Ransom, Blackmur and Brooks paid serious attention to poetic diction but as they had no idea of the findings of modern linguistics, they never thought of reality-in-text. The American critics considered a poem either an imitation or a verbal icon.

The first systematic study of literature in the light of modern linguistics began in Russia when Roman Jakobson founded the Moscow Linguistic Circle in 1915 and Viktor Shklovsky the Society for the study of Poetic Language (Opoyaz) in 1916. Although the two groups did not collaborate, yet they shared a common ground for the study of literature. They all agreed to establish a study of literature on scientific basis and make formal and linguistic analysis to determine what makes literariness and distinguishes it from other modes of discourse, especially the prosaic and ordinary language. Since they — Roman Jakobson, Jurij Tynyanov, Viktor Shklovsky and Boris Eichenbaum — aimed at specifying the formal and linguistic properties of literature, they called themselves specifiers.

As they developed their poetics on the basics of linguistics, it will be pertinent to correlate De Saussure's concepts of (a) signifier and signified, (b) phone and phoneme, (c) langue and parole, and (d) diachronic and synchronic studies of language with their concepts of literature, literary text, literary criticism and literary history.

The relationship between the signifier and the signified is arbitrary, that is, there is no logical relationship between a sign and the concept it refers to; the signifier *cat* for example, refers to the concept of the cat, not the object, and the relationship between the two is based on convention. Closely related to it is the concept of phoneme, the smallest unit in the sound system of a language. A speech sound (phone) becomes a phoneme in a language in its contrastive relationship with the other speech sounds in that language. For example the speech sound |b| is a phoneme in English because it is in contrast with other phonemes in the language. From this follows that all the units of a language derive their meaning from their mutual relationship in a system. The Formalists, on the basis of the first concept, challenged the mimetic theory. They argued if words are signifiers of concepts and we come to know concepts through words, literature, which is basically a linguistic structure, is a signifier of reality. There is, of course, the world of reality but we know that world through the mediation of words or language. In other words, the reality we comprehend in a literary text is embedded in the text itself.

Following the concept of phoneme that it exists because of its difference with other phonemes, they concluded that a text exists in contrast with other texts in the literary system and derives its meaning from its mutual relationships with them.

Coming to the nature and function of criticism they followed the concept of *langue* and *parole*. De Saussure defined *langue* as the system of language and *parole* as individual speech acts. Tynyanov and Jakobson accepted the great linguist's emphasis on the study of langue as it is limited and is the key factor of language and on that pattern argued that the primary concern of criticism is to study the literary text, not biography, history of ideas, sociology or religion. They laid emphasis on the fact that it is the duty of literary criticism to trace or describe the principles that work in the composition of a literary work as a particular kind of discourse.

Finally, they maintained, on the basis of Saussure's division of diachromic and synchromic study of language, that it is beyond the jurisdiction of literary criticism to study the historical development and, so, literary criticism should concentrate on the text itself and should not consider the historical or biographical reasons for its structural analysis. As such literary criticism is essentially ahistorical and it is the task of literary history to study the historical development of literature. Eichenbaum declared :

> "The study of literary genetics can classify only the origin of a device nothing more; poetics must serve different functions in different literary texts" (FM 52).

Roman Jakobson as late as in 1958 repeated his contemporary :

> "Literary studies, with poetics as their focal portion, consist like linguistics of two sets of problems : Synchrony and diachrony. The synchronic description envisages not only the literary production of any given stage but also that part of the literary tradition which for the stage in question has remained vital or has been revived.... A thoroughly comprehensive historical poetics or history of language is a superstructure to be built on a series of successive description" (MCT 34).

After making a distinction between literary history and literary criticism, the Formalists contended that the study of literature should become an autonomous science having its principles, and techniques of its own. In the words of Tony Bennett,

> "Such a science would need first to specify the nature of the object to which it would address itself, to state clearly what it was to be a science of and to map out clearly the conceptual space it would occupy" (FM 48).

The Formalists first took up the literary text and then tried to define literature contrasting it with other discourses. Here they followed Saussurian principle of contrast. Since a literary text stands in contrast with other texts in the system of literature, the task of criticism is to determine the inter-relationship between texts and trace the principle of their composition. The main problem, they said, is to make distinction between the literary and non-literary and, therefore, to quote Jakobson,

> "The real field of literary science is not literature but literariness, in other words, that which makes a work literary" (FM 55).

Jakobson enumerated six functions of language : referential, emotive, poetic, conative, phatic and metalingual, and said that :

> "The poetic function projects the principle of equivalence from the axis of selection into the axis of combination" (MCT 39).

Shklovsky considered the device of "defamiliarisation" as the main feature to divide the literary from the non-literary. In the famous essay "Art as Technique" he wrote :

> "The purpose of art is to impart the sensation of things as they are perceived, and not as they are known. The technique or art is to make objects "unfamiliar", to make forms difficult, to increase the difficulty and length of perception because the process of perception is aesthetic and in itself and must be prolonged. Art is a way of experiencing the artfulness of an object; the object is not important" (MCT 20).

In his brilliant analysis of Tolstoy's technique he used the terms "defamiliarise" and "defamiliarisation" :

> "Tolstoy makes the familiar seem strange by not naming the familiar object. He describes an object as it he were seeing it for the first time, an event as if it were happening for the first time. In describing something he avoids the accepted names of its parts and instead names corresponding parts of other objects. For example in 'Shame' Tolstoy 'defamiliarises' the idea of flogging... Tolstoy uses this technique of 'defamiliarisation' constantly" (MCT 21).

Boris Eichenbaum used the term "bestrangement" while analysing Tolstoy's *Sevastopol Sketches*. The term is a noun derived from the root "strange" with the addition of the prefix "be" and suffix "ment" and means the condition of being unfamiliar or strange. Both Shklovsky and Eichenbaum made distinction between *fabula* (the raw material) and *sjuzet* (the plot). They considered a literary text a transformation of the reality perceived by the writer into a code and the main device used for transformation is the technique of defamiliarisation or bestrangement.

The great contribution of the Formalist critics was that they made literary criticism as objective as science and opened a new vista to the study of literature. Certainly they were the first to employ the findings of linguistics to the study of literature and make literary criticism autonomous. But the matter did not end here. The French structuralists carried the tradition further.

The famous article "Problems in the Study of Literature" by Tynyanov and Jakobson is widely considered to be the foundation stone of structuralism. While in Russia they were developing their aesthetic principles, they found little time to pay attention to the relation between art and social structure. After October Revolution Jakobson emigrated from the USSR and founded the Prague School of linguistics. He came in contact with Claude Levi-Strauss, a great French anthropologist. Both in collaboration analysed Baudelaire's "Les Chats". From here began the French structuralism. Levi-Strauss propounded that all human activities should be viewed as being organised like a language. Applying Saussure's concept of *langue* and *parole* in his anthropological studies he analysed and interpreted ancient myths, numbering more than eight hundred, and concluded that all myths are related structures and are formal transformation of one another.

While interpreting myths and analysing mythical thought Levi-Strauss used two terms : *bricolage* and *bricoleur*. According to him *bricolage* is the art of making things from the existing materials and the existing tools and *bricoleur* is the person who reconstructs out of the existing materials with the help of the tools that are within his reach. In other words, he is not an engineer who invents new tools. The myth-maker is a *bricoleur* who reconstructs the myth he has access to and mythical thought is a kind of intellectual *bricolage* (See TCC 442).

Gerard Gennette in his lucid essay "Structuralism and Literary Criticism" (1964) refers to Levi-Strauss' concept of engineer and *bricoleur* and quotes the following sentence :

> "(The engineer) questions the universe, while the bricoleur addresses himself to a collection of oddments left over from human endeavours, that is, only a subset of culture" (MCT 64).

Then he comments that the creative writer can be substituted for engineer and the critic for the *bricoleur* to define the status of literary criticism. The creative write, while questioning the universe builds a structure. The *bricoleur* or the critic breaks down the structure into its elements — one element per card — and next he builds up a new structure" (MCT 66).

In other words the critic's task is to break the literary text into structural units and then restructure them into a new structure. He must not add anything extra from his side; on the other hand he "must make it possible to uncover the connection that exists between a system of forms and a system of meanings, by replacing the search for term-by-term analysis with one for overall homologues" (MCT 66).

It is not enough for him to study the structure of poetic language and the forms of literary expression, he has also to analyse the relation between code and message.

The limitation of Formalism was that it narrowed itself to the confines of textual study. Gerard Gennette comments that structuralism released literary criticism from the blind alley of Formalism which considered literature as a mere dialect.

"Literature being primarily a work of language, and structuralism, for its part, being pre-eminently a linguistic method, the most probable encounter should obviously take place on the terrain of linguistic material; sounds, forms, words and sentences constitute the common object of the linguist and the philologist to such an extent that it was possible in the early enthusiasm of the Russian Formalist movement, to define literature as a mere dialect, and to envisage its study as an annex of general dialectology" (MCT 65).

Although it is difficult to agree with this estimate of the Russian Formalist movement (Jakobson, Tynyanov, even Shklovsky never considered literature a mere dialect), yet it is clear from this passage that structuralist critics accepted their inheritance of the Russian Formalism which is rightly regarded as one of the matrices of structural linguistics.

Structuralist criticism came to its maturity through Roland Barthes who is generally accepted as the greatest post-structuralist critic. Structuralism gave social edifice to literary criticism but not history, nor ideology. Roland Barthes, basically Saussurian, combined philosophy, history and sociology together for the study of literature. He created a stir in the British and American literary circle by his essay "Criticism as Language" published in the second of the two special issues of *The Times Literary Supplement* (1963).

He begins the essay by mentioning the main critical trends in France, namely, Existentialism, Marxism, Psycho-analysis and Structuralism. Being a great admirer of Jean Paul Sartre, who had tried to combined Marxism and Existentialism, he makes ideology as one of the most important elements of criticism. He says :

> "Criticism is something other than making correct statements in the light of "true" principles. It follows that the major sin in criticism is not to have an ideology but to keep quiet about it" (TCLC 648-49).

After ideology comes the relationship between the author and the work. Here Barthes is closely connected to psycho-analysis, Marxism and Existentialism.

"Criticism is not in any sense a table of results or a body of judgements; it is essentially an activity, that is to say a series of intellectual acts inextricably involved with the historical and subjective (the two terms are synonymous) existence of the person who carries them out and has to assume responsibility for them" (TCLC 649).

Thirdly, Barthes adopts the postulates of structuralism and says that literature is a linguistic structure, a semiotic organization of signification, which deals with the universe and criticism is a comment on the linguistic structure. In other words criticism is a meta-language that explains the object language, the language of literature. Criticism therefore takes two kinds of relationship into account : the first is "the relationship between the critical language and the language of the author under consideration" and the second is "the relationship between the latter (language-as-object) and the world" (TCLC 649).

It is this dual relationship that defines criticism and brings it near to logic which is "entirely founded on the distinction between language-as-object and meta-language". As logic is concerned with validity (language can be either valid or non-valid), criticism is concerned with validity, not truth. "We might say", writes Barthes,

> "that the task of criticism (and this is the only guarantee of its universality) is purely formal; it does not consist in "discovering" something "hidden" or "profound" or "secret" which has so far escaped notice (through what miracle? Are we more perceptive than our predecessors?) but only in fitting together...the language of the day (Existentialism, Marxism or psycho-analysis) and the language of the author..." (TCTL 650).

Coming to the relationship between literature and criticism, Barthes says that criticism is a formal activity in the logical sense of the term, not in the aesthetic sense and literature is "neither ever quite meaningless (mysterious or inspired) nor ever quite clear, it is, so to speak, suspended meaning, it offers itself to the reader as a declared system of significance, but as a signified object it eludes his grasp" (TCTL 650). It is also that literature is a very "special semantic system" and its aim is "to put meaning into the world but not a meaning" (TCTL 650-51).

It is this typical nature of literature that invites literary criticism to be formal like logic and to have base in linguistics. The function of criticism is to reconstitute the system and determine the formal structure. Barthes concludes :

> "Literature, since it consists at one and the same time of the insistent offering of a meaning and the persistent elusiveness of that meaning, is definitely no more than a language, that is, a system of signs; its being lies not in the message but in the system. This being so, the critic is not called upon to reconstitute the message of the work, but only its system, just as the business of the linguist is not to decipher the meaning of a sentence but

to determine the formal structure which permits the transmission of its meaning" (TCLC 650-51).

It is roughly on this theoretical foundation that Barthes analyses Balzac's "Sarrasine" and Poe's "Valdemar". He accepts Claude Levi-Strauss' notion of structure and structural analysis, but makes the modification that structural analysis is applied to above all oral narrative (*i.e.* myth) and textual analysis exclusively to written narrative. Textual analysis does not try to describe the structure of a work, although it follows the structural principles; its main task is to produce 'a mobile structuration of the text (a structuration which is displaced from reader to reader throughout history), of staying in the signifying volume of the work, in its significance. Textual analysis does not try to find out what it is that determines the text...but rather how the text explodes and disperses..." (MCT 174).

The procedure to be followed is first to divide the text into lexias (lexie), very short linguistic units, which can be a sentence, part of a sentence, or at most a group of three or four sentences. The next step is to observe the meanings to which the texias give rise. Here the aim is not to find the meaning or even a meaning but to manage to perceive the plurality of the text, the opening of its significance. The reading is like a slow-film or unfolding the pages slowly to follow the structure.

Barthes almost echoes Hopkins. It is to be noted that Jakobson and Barthes both were influenced by Hopkins's theory of poetry.

Finally, we have to consider departures of meanings, not arrivals. Barthes writes :

> "What founds the text is not an internal, closed, recountable structure but the outlet of the text on to other texts, other signs; what makes the text intertextual" (MCT 174).

The departures of meaning can be best deciphered in the cultural code of which all other are sub-species. To conclude, Barthes' methodology is essentially structural or formal but he takes into account the existentialist, marxist and psycho-analytical ideologies. His view of a text is certainly of a linguist, but the linguist has an ideology and his structuration of the text is always in a cultural context.

Jonathan Culler and Richard Ohmann, both American critics, need mention. Both have employed Chomsky's T.G. Grammar in the analysis of a literary text. Jonathan Culler is more theoretical in his approach and the analyses he has made of Blake's "London" and of William Carlos Williams' poem in the article "Structuralism and Literature" is not very different from those of Leavis, Brooks and Olson except the terms used such as "the symbolic code", "the artificiality of literature", "strangeness" and "signs". He himself admits that the interpretation of a poem may not be significantly different from what is revealed by a more conventional kind of analysis. What is significant, he affirms, is that it makes explicit the processes we take for granted.

Richard Ohmann employs Chomsky's transformational rules as given in *Syntactic Structures* and *Aspects of the Theory of Syntax*. In his analysis of the Victorian prose he writes that the thought process take place at the level of deep structure and finds its expression at the surface structure through a set of transformational rules. The same kernel sentence can generate different kinds of sentences and a writer while writing a literary piece makes stylistic choices. "The stylistic choices", to quote his own words, "operating among alternate formulations of prepositional content form a pattern...that implies a characteristic way of conceiving, relating and presenting content" (294).

Towards the end of the essay "A Linguistic Appraisal of Victorian Style" he like the structuralists, gives due importance to the role of culture in shaping a writer's mind and like Barthes accepts the importance of history.

"A man who occupies a given spot in history and culture is urged by his intellectual world to think and feel in certain ways, but the forming power of intellectual culture operates on a mind already formed, deeply and intricately, by a thousand sub-cultures, from the nursery on up. Style is responsive to the cut of a writer's mind, and that is only trimmed and decorated by intellectual culture, not created by it" (308).

He also favours the synchronic study like De Saussure, the Formalists and the Structuralists. He closes the essay with the following remarks :

> "Those of us interested in Victorian prose style will do well to study individual writers intensively, and with the best linguistic theory available to discover the unique and intriguing shapes that mind and language take among the Victorians.... Reliable judgements about the history of style will come after an understanding of styles, and may be quite other than what the textbooks say" (309).

It was difficult to assess the influence of linguistics on the study of literature in the fifties or early sixties in Britain and America. Now younger critics are using the findings of modern linguistics in analysing literary texts and defining literature and literary criticism and its function. In India, linguistics and literature are yet to be combined. Roman Jakobson in his "Closing Statement" to a conference on "Style in Language" held at Indiana University in 1958, later on, published under the title "Linguistics and Poetics", concluded thus :

> "All of us here, however, definitely realize that a linguist deaf to the poetic function of language and a literary scholar indifferent to linguistic problems and unconversant with linguistic methods are equally flagrant anachronisms" (MCT 55).

Perhaps, this advice of Jakobson is most relevant in Indian context today.

WORKS CITED

Bennett, Tony, *Formalism and Marxism*. London and New York : Methuen, 1979. Cited as FM.

Handy, William J. and Max Westbrook, Eds., *Twentieth Century Criticism : Major Statements*. New Delhi : Light and Life Publishers, 1976. Cited as TCC.

Lodge, David, Ed., *Modern Criticism and Theory*. London : Longman, 1988. Cited as MCT.

——, *20th Century Literary Criticism*. London and New York : Longman, 1972. Quotations are from 1985 impression.

Ohmann, Richard, "A Linguistic Appraisal of Victorian Style". In *The Art of Victorian Prose*. Eds. George Levine and William Madden. New York : Oxford University Press, 1968.

14

Stylistics : An Overview

—Mallikarjun Patil

STYLISTICS is a discipline of literature. What linguistics is to language, stylistics is to literature. In fact, stylistics is the 'science of literature'; it is an objective study of its texts, or an interpretation of linguistic embellishments of language used in literature. There is a certain inherent rapport between linguistics and stylistics. However, stylistics as a discipline, has its own origin, growth, nature and scope. It concerns itself with the linguistic interpretation of literary text. In the words of Enkvist, the task of stylistics is "to set up inventories and descriptions of stylistic stimuli with the aid of linguistic concepts". In tune with linguistics, the methods of stylistics are clearly objective. In this regard, stylistics stands apart from the discipline of literary criticism, especially traditional criticism which is subjective.

As mentioned above, the origin and growth of stylistics is not remote to seek. So this discipline is of a recent growth, though its origin is remote. In fact, stylistics began as a subject in 1950's with a series of fresh starts. Even as a separate discipline it has not yet found a place in many universities today. Besides, there are no readymade textbooks available save a few editions of articles on the subject. In addition to this no proper perspective about the strengths and limitations of the subject are seriously attempted so far.

Stylistics which arose as a handmaid to literary criticism aims at studying literary texts as objectively as possible. It does not take care of details pertaining to the author, the period, or the other extratextual data on which traditional criticism so much relied, in this regard there is a very close relationship between stylistics and Russian formalism, French structuralism and New Criticism. Linguistics plays a role here in as much as the stylistician analyses the details that are missed or neglected by the literary critic. In this connection, we should not think stylistics — a discipline created to replace the traditional literary criticism. Stylistics merely plays a subordinate role here. So stylistics is not a superior discipline to literary criticism. Here both the stylistician and the critic have a duty of complementary nature and they need to work together in the interpretation of a literary text. In the words of M.I. Shastri the stylistician assists the critic in his attempts at explication, without any sense of condescension, while the critic is grateful to the other who supplies supporting evidences from the text for his intuitive judgements. However, stylistics, M.I. Shastri remarks, has something concrete to go by in the textual features whereas criticism chooses to ignore the text at hand totally in deference to the author's biography or the theme's analogues.

Here I have tried to give certain details regarding the origin, growth, nature and scope of stylistics, as an individual discipline. This article aims at providing details regarding the historical antecedents of stylistics, a few theories of style, and the current trends on the matter. An information regarding the application of stylistics to the teaching of literature is also provided. And a few of Indian views on style are given too in contrast to the Western views on the matter.

Although the growth of stylistics as a new subject was felt in 1960 with the publication of *Style in Language*, it has an antique origin. Aristotle had, long ago, said that style is part of rhetoric and not poetics. According to him vocabulary, syntax and figures of speech are aimed at producing a certain effect on the audience. In his work *Institute of Oratory*, Quintilian (Ist century A.D.) too said the same things which firmly found their effect in the European thought till the modern times. In his celebrated essay "Discourse on Style", Comte de Buffon (1707-1788) viewed style as a means to a rhetorical end. As a result, it was inferred that style is an ordering process of writing. Later the views of Ferdinand de Saussure (1857-1913), Charles Bally (1865-1947) and Leo Spitzer (1887-1960) gave a fresh impetus to the growth of the subject. Spitzer made a research on literary stylistics and stated that criticism should deal with the work as much without any preconceived notions of *a priori* judgement. According to him, after reading a work many times over, a critic can grasp the 'spiritual etymon' by an intuitive 'click' and thereafter understand its inner order. This hypothesis led him to establish the notion of 'philological circle'. In course of time Saussurean structuralism influenced Roman Jakobson, Jan Mukarovsky and René Welleck, the practitioners of Prague School (circle linuistique de prage). These linguists expressed the view that the formal features of creative utterances can be studied objectively to understand their operation in some general way. So the Prague School served as an important link between literary criticism and linguistic stylistics. Afterwards the structuralists like Edward Sapir (1884-1939) and Leonard Bloomfield (1887-1949) thought that their approach to literature "subordinates aspects of surface structure in favour of an investigation of some deeper, more abstract patterns which govern the inner form of the work". It is affirmed stylistics "emphasizes particularity, individuality, concreteness" and "makes the individual work more recognizable, more discrete, its physiognomy more salient". While Claude Levi-Strauss elaborated the view that literature combines the features of anthropology and linguistics, and the fundamental principle of human thinking is 'binary opposition'.

Practical criticism originated by I.A. Richards in 1930's was a new step that gave a new insight to the growth of stylistics. In his practical criticism, I.A. Richards reinforced the close reading of the texts and he paid no attention to the historical and geographical details of the texts. This paved a way to the New Criticism which, in turn, brought us to the threshold of modern stylistics.

New Criticism that was begun with John Crowe Ransom's publication *New Criticism* (1941) expounded the view that the poem is a 'legitimate object of study in itself', 'a monumental thing-in-itself', and a unique but highly-ordered 'organism'. Description for its own sake was not practised by the New Critics. So New Criticism and Structuralism emphasized objective study of the texts. While René Wellek and Austin Warren pointed out that literature is a linguistic art and language is its raw material at all levels. Besides, the formulations of Transformational Generative Grammar by Noam Chomsky and book *Style in Language* (1960), published by the members of Social Science Research Council of Indiana University opened up new ways of handling and laying bare the internal working of language.

However, linguistic approach to literature also existed side by side. Many linguists felt that since the language was the stuff of which literature was made, linguistics should be able to comment on it in a sensible way, of course, without affecting the value judgements. In this regard Harold Whitehall went a step further and affirmed that as no science can go beyond mathematics, no criticism can go beyond its linguistics". These bold studies of stylistics strengthened the linguistic approach of it. Michael Halliday put it effectively that "there is no text without style". Jan Mukarovsky opined "all literary language is a purposeful distortion of ordinary language". This led Nils Erik Enkvist to consolidate and express his view that "the style of a text is the aggregate of the contextual probabilities of its linguistic items".

According to the Prague linguists, the central notion of style is called 'foregrounding'. The opposite of foregrounding is automatization which is a process by which a previously foregrounded expression loses its aesthetic value for later readers. Here foregrounding serves as an attention-calling device in a literary passage through the use of repetition, emphasis, unexpected lexical collocations, syntactic inversions etc. While the structuralist school of linguistics maintained that style could simply be studied as the difference between synonymous sentences. According to the British school of linguistics of

J.R. Firth and M.A.K. Halliday language is presented as a system containing several sub-systems. These linguists emphasise the aspects of register, field, mode, context, unit, structure, class and system. Of the various linguistic descriptions of style, the one based on transformational generative grammar has commanded a greater respect over the years. Accordingly surface structure which represents performance and belongs to the domain of style in given much consideration. Richard Ohmann with this technique analysed G.B. Shaw's style. He found that frequent use of relativization, conjuction and comparison characterize Faulkner's style. In Ohman's view, Henry James used a good deal of embedding and D.H. Lawrence's style is built on deletion. In all these linguistic approaches to the analysis of texts, style is identified, in the words of Roger Fowler, "as the sum of a number of points on several linguistic scales". Even the shortest utterance can be analysed with respect to a number of linguistic features. An ordinary sentence like 'what a beautiful day!' assumes different kinds of stylistic significance depending upon the tone of the speaker, weather of the day etc. So the situation is much complex in the case of a literary text. A variety of features, for example in the case of this sentence, the tone, the weather of the day, the stress etc., are called 'convergence'. Which characterizes the style of a writer. Similarly Halliday and Hasan use the notion of cohesion in stylistic analysis. Here cohesive features may be either grammatical (*e.g.* use of determiners, pronouns, demonstratives, certain adverbs) or lexical (*e.g.* repetition of words, sequential occurrence of items from a given lexical set).

Thus these approaches to the study of stylistics indicate three current trends *i.e.* (1) style as a deviation, (2) style, as convergence of textual patterns, and (3) style, a result of a particular exploitation of a grammar of possibilities. When we think style as a conceptual deviance, we mean that the poet or writer deviates from the norm even when he conceives something in his mind and later he commits it to the paper. Let it be borne in mind that all great literature is a product of conceptual deviance. In this regard, the poetry or any form, of literature if it really deviates from grammaticality, may or may not be acceptable. For example, "anyone lived in a pretty how town" is tolerated in the context of Cumming's poem. But the following lines of conceptual deviance are not accepted :

(a) a who the of today (violation of the basic syntactic rule of English).
(b) I thermometer you (use of noun in place of verb).
(c) I elapsed the book to her (elapse is unsuitable).
(d) The stone snores (no animate noun).

But the following sentence from *Moby Dick* which shows conceptual deviation is accepted :

> And heaved and heaved, still unrestingly heaved the black sea, as it its vast tides were a conscience.

In the light of the above analysis, deviance can thus be redefined as the "difference between a text and the overall grammatical norm of the language" and "the sum of non-grammaticality and nonacceptability". Besides, a conceptual deviance is metaphorical in nature, and it leads to a greater creativity. Anyway there are degrees of deviance which are closely related to degrees of grammaticality. We can also say that the more grammatical a sentence, is the less creative (deviant) it is, with an attendent quantum of banality (alternatives).

When we consider the style of poetry, the importance of stylistic study will be known to us. As most of us know the language of poetry is something quite different from the language of prose though William Wordsworth reacted against this. Accordingly the language of poetry is something that arouses aesthetic imagination (Owen Barfield), 'is a special selection' (Josephine Miles, Donald Davie), is different from the language of age (Tennyson) etc. But the definition of poetic language given by Jan Mukarovsky of Prague School is excellent : "Poetic language is the distortion of the ordinary language". This is done for the sake of foregrounding which creates an aesthetic effect and an ever-lasting impression. Poetic language is a

'Separate language', 'a dialect of the standard' and it has its own style. It has a special Vocabulary and different combinations of its own. Poetic language is different from the prose language mainly for the purpose of foregrounding which is done for engaging the reader's intellect. So poetry uses highly patterned and organized mode of expressions. Look at Steven Orien's "Country House" :

> The house is old, too small to contain lives furnished with smog, to, divorce. The trees I drag like errant children from the hills are squandered in the fire place.

The beginning is direct, but the comparison of trees with errant children and fuel with money is unique in the poem. This is done for the purpose of foregrounding. So here the deviance is quite conceptual. The strong reason as to why distorted language is employed by poets is to achieve an ever lasting poetic effect that remains forever. Paul Valery states :

> The poem, on the other hand, does not die for having lived : it is expressly designed to be born again from its ashes and to become endlessly what it has just been. Poetry can be recognized by this property, that it tends to got itself reproduced in its own forms : it stimulates us to reconstruct it identically.

Similarly in case of prose passages, there is no need for a complete inventory of linguistic features; just the salient ones will do to account for its effect. Then it is very useful. In M.I. Sastri's views, to what register the passage belongs is based on the field of discourse (*e.g.* journalism, advertisement, science, literature, law, etc.) and the style of discourse (*e.g.* formal, informal, consultative, etc.). The lexis and syntax provide us the principle clues to this stylistic analysis of the prose pieces.

Since stylistics is regarded as applied linguistics, it is used in teaching of literature too. This helps teachers to help their students appreciate the artistic use of language and enhance their linguistic competence. In Envist's opinion, this is helpful to students in acquiring sense of style. Stylistic approach in teaching literature enriches students' aesthetic qualities in regard to their understanding also. They learn the role of language in understanding a text with ease and grace. In stylistic analysis, literature is presented as dynamic communication, not mechanically a response to a stimulus, but something triggering a spontaneous interaction between the text and reader. In his work *Stylistics and the Teaching of Literature* (1975), H.G. Widdowson examines the nature of literary communication and stylistics as an exercise in literary understanding. So this is enough for our understanding of stylistics in teaching literature.

In regard to the theories of style, though not a profound study is undertaken, sufficient knowledge is unearthed. Broadly speaking there are three theories of style *i.e.* style as dress of thought, style as an organism, and style as the man. According to the first theory both the matter and manner can be separated. Here style is an embellishment or ornament to the content, hence divisible from the other. Puttenham, and Lord Chesterfield supported this view. They observe that a text can have different kinds of styles (dress) for different occasions. Consequently, the concepts of grand, plain and bombastic styles were framed and discussed.

But the Romantic poets like Coleridge and Wordsworth did not accept style as a dress of thoughts. Instead, they expressed the view that style is inseparable from the thought. This theory of them is known as 'organic theory of style'. Later Herbert Read and the New Critics practised this view. To Romantics, style is more than the dress of thoughts. The mind is the art making organism. There can be no kind of divorce between language and thought. To Wordsworth the figures of speech or any other stylistic features appeared not as "billiard balls" but as molecules. These outside features contribute to the total effect. Poetry to Wordsworth was truth "carried alive into the heart of passion". Similarly, Coleridge affirms, "They (images) become proofs of original genius only as far as they are modified by a predominant passion". In the organic view, intuition is nothing but expression. Newman says "style is thinking out into language", while

Archibald MacLeish states "a poem should not mean but be.... It is autonomous".

The third theory is psychologically-oriented. It is illustrated in the well-known definition of Buffon that 'style is the man'. In this we try to attribute certain habits of language to certain character traits in the man. But this theory is unacceptable because man writes differently on different occasions. For evidence a man's talk with others will be varied. In the case of his students, wife, children, friends and kindred. So are his modes of writing.

There are many approaches to style originated both in India and the West. Bhamaha (6th century), a Sankrit poet says that poetry is the togetherness of sound and sense which view corroborates the organic theory of style. Bhamaha defines poetry as *Śabdarthau Sahitau Kāvyam (Kāvyalaṁkār)* which is similar to Paul Valery's definition of poetry that "in poetry the form and content are indissolubly united in wedlock" ("Poetry and Abstract Thought", *Art of Poetry*).

However, Bhamaha emphasises more on sound or embellishment which has the effect due to its *vakrokti* or deviance from the normal language. Dandin, a contemporary of Bhamaha, emphasises both on sound and sense which together suggest an elegant idea. So Bhamaha and Dandin reinforce more on the body of poetry than on its soul. But Vaman's emphasis is on the soul of poetry instead. He says style is the soul of poetry. While Anandavardhana of Kashmir (9th century) and Abhinavagupta give much importance *dhrani* or suggestion of poetry. The Indian critics of poetics on the basis of *rasa* theory classify poetry into three kinds *i.e.* poetry, verse and the middle one that is either equal or inferior to the other two. But Kuntak (10th century) affirms that poetry is *Vakrokti* or deviance which is similar to Makarovasky's view of poetic language. Kshemendra (11th century) of Kashmir, says *aucitya* or propriety is the life of poetry and *rasa* (suggestion) is its soul. *Aucitya* is nothing but coherence and unity of the theme and treatment of the embellishments in a poem, So Indian approaches to style are as varied as their Western counterparts.

The importance of stylistics for the study, judgement and evaluation of a text is very much in consideration of subjective criticism. But stylistics as a discipline is not yet totally self-sufficient or reliable. So the fate of stylistics today is a declining one. Only people like historicists and feminists best use the discipline to solve their problems, whereas critics do not exploit it to its fullest extent. No doubt the demerits of stylistics, as a study, are glaring and inconvenient.

15

The Panchkriya Theory of Criticism and Hamlet

—*A.K. Awasthi*

AT the crossroad of philosophical view and advancing scientific explanations of cosmic activity ancient Indian theory of the Dance of Shiva and *Trika darshan* have not only acquired significance but also received scientific rationale. Fritjof Capra, a modern physicist explaining the nature of subatomic matter has drawn a parallel between Shiva's dance and cosmic activity. He declares, "Shiva's dance is the dance of subatomic matter." The bubble-chamber photographs of rhythm of creation and destruction in the universe are visual images of the dance of Shiva. Other physicists like Kenneth Ford and Heinrich Zimmer also speak about 'energy dance' or 'dance of creation and destruction' that leads to acknowledge the fundamental principle of balance in all forms of nature. The String theory of physics is claimed to be the theory of everything that resolves the incompatibility of quantum mechanics and relativity and states "that matter and force are simply different aspects of the same fundamental entity and are thus unified.... All particles arise as different vibrations of the same elementary string". Similarly, the *Trika darshan* holds the triad principle as fundamental — *Shiva, Shakti* and identity of both.

The *Panchkriya* principle is derived from the same fundamental, that describes five eternal activities attributed to Shiva who is in the state of eternal dance, and therefore is manifest in the form of cosmic activities that can be described as the dance of Nature and wisdom of soul in gross terms. Shiva is not a god in person; it is a name given to the fundamental principle, which means 'all light' (*prakash, i.e.* truth) including the good and the beautiful. As Panchkriya is universal in nature, it can be well applied to any limited activity in order to explain and evaluate such proposition.

There is an unidentified order in the universe. In *Trika darshan* it is described as Shiva's nature (*swabhavajaha*). One may call it natural order or reason. All forms — animate and inanimate — are only charged particles of natural reason. The five activities are only states/aspects intrinsic to everything in nature. Panchkriyas, therefore, are formidably potent to explain any artistic or another activity which is only a form of cosmic activity. The five states are :

Creation (*srishti*) — will or inspiration to create;

Preservation/sustenance (*stithi*) — to uphold and follow the course of thought;

Transformation/destruction (*samhar*) — to dismiss or disintegrate all that is not inconsonance with the natural order (*i.e.* Shiva), to purify thought and/or transform and take a new form;

Diffusion of illusion (*tirobhava*) — identification with the approach and vision of reality; and

Attaining Grace (*anugraha*) — identity with the subject (*Aham*) and object (*idam*), sublimated thought or truth revealed.

In the poetic/artistic creation similar activities are evident. As in the cosmos, so in a work of art, Nature or poet (Shiva) wills it to happen, which is the natural rationale, so the activity (*shakti*) gets started. It is a free movement, upward or downward, rightward or leftward. Eternal consciousness is known as bliss in gross terms, which in the most comprehensive sense is known as will, which again in wider application becomes knowledge (*jnana*). It is this knowledge that results in the grossest form of consciousness, that is, in the state of activity in Shiva or any artist who in turn automatically activates the panchkriya principle and the process of artistic activity starts. It continues until the objective has been gained. It is this process that takes place in the mind of the poet before any actual activity gets a form, direction, colour, etc. A critic therefore has to understand first the mental processing of the object of inspiration (but it would be better to call it "subject" of inspiration for the inspiration takes place only within) leading to actual artistic production. He can do so by getting to know the (near) totality of the environment, the poet has lived. Quality in the work will descend on its own spontaneously through Panchkriyas.

The Lord of the Universe is dancing the cycle of grace in the form of perfect balance — *Ardhanarishwara*, which is known as the balance of Nature, so does the poet. Any one who gains this balance in any sphere of activity attains the vision as a state of evolution/realization, which is qualified by solemn, serene and sublime feel of the cosmic reality that is expressed in words pregnant with truth, its extent, intensity and feeling — THE BALANCE OF ALL. The poet as well as the critic displays reason as a tool that does all the analysing and evaluation. The method of assessment of quality follows the rule of consonance of abilities between the poet and the reader/critic and diffusion of infirmities (attachment-drains) in the work of art. These are five in all. If the poet has been conscious to art, knowledge, attachment, time and destiny (*i.e. kala, vidya, kaal, rag* and *niyati*), his work is bound to have the tendency of backward pull, that, no doubt, leads to ambiguity of meaning and interpretations. For the upward scale, the following table displays the process of creating perfect art :

Evolution from —

Limited skill — to — all skill

Little knowledge — to — all knowledge

Desire or awareness to achieve — to — fulfilment

Specific time — to — timelessness

Limited sphere activity — to — widespread activity.

In other words, a perfect artistic activity exhibits an ascending order : art leads to realization of truth; knowledge is replaced by enlightenment; life of attachment gives way to emergence of will and subjectivity to time changes into universal appeal and belief in destiny is transformed as total activity. This is what the poet becomes in the mind. The *Trika darshan* mentions these as (five mouths) five modes of expression of Shiva, the Lord of the universe. In the poet these are known to be the qualities of an unpolluted mind — free and content, willing (to create), enlightened and prone to activity. Only a mind possessing these qualities can be said to be the most appropriate ground for creating a work of art. In the poet the triad principle is represented as a process : (1) drive to realize truth or discover (Shiva), followed by (2) ensuing activity (*shakti*), (3) to attain the contentment of the soul (the identity of both). Thus, Panchkriya is a perfect principle that can evaluate any work of art as well as any human activity.

Evil is a phenomenon in Shakespeare's tragedies. It is part of thinking material. All is evil that has the power to harm others' interest. The conception reflects a pattern of thought and a scheme too. The whole thing undergoes a process of gradual development. It begins with Hamlet's famous exclamation, "what a piece of work is man! How noble in reason! How like god!" Polonius has already noted that too much thinking may lead to madness yet 'there is a method in it' (II, ii, 210). The emphasis is on reason, which is followed by a smalltime experiment in OTHELLO, wherein unreason affects lives of Othello and Desdemona. KING LEAR illustrates a large-scale flare-up and repercussions of evil, which kills the good, *i.e.* Cordelia with little redeeming sentiments except consolation, which the audience feels at the end. In MACBETH evil is displayed at its maximum scale. It engulfs the whole country. The symbol of goodness (Duncan) is eliminated in the beginning and the hero turns into a villain. It is followed by reign of terror caused by unreason. It is finally destroyed and the good is restored but at the cost of good only. Such configuration in Shakespeare's tragedy points to a consistency of pattern, which lies in the underlying principle — the conflict of opposites, reason and unreason.

The Indian esthetical (aesthetic) standard as enunciated by Abhinavgupta and elaborated by Anand Coomaraswamy under the *Dance of Shiva* prescribes the fundamentals of literary criticism/evaluation which are in complete harmony with the natural principle, and are derived from a holistic principle known as triad under the TRIKA DARSAN — *prakasa (light), vimarsa (self-consciousness),* and their union also known as *spand (vibration).* Other parallels are Shiva, Uma and their identity-in-consciousness, *i.e.* will, knowledge or action and the manifested or manifestable; the individual, knowledge and the known; buddhi, application of buddhi and manifestation.

The phenomenon is three-dimensional. In HAMLET and OTHELLO unreason of any action is : (1) substratum that gives rise to psychic images (or buddhi as it would act) *i.e.* the guiding light or *prakasa*; (2) design or scheme of thought that makes the actor self-conscious of his being and preparedness for action is vimarsa; (3) objective gained by the playwright, *i.e.* resolution of the theme as manifestation or union of the two. Such premise is developed from application of the Indian aesthetical principles of plays question.

The Cosmic Activity is the central motif of the Dance, which is eternal and universal. It implies that the Lord of the Universe is the 'Dancer who like fire latent in firewood, diffuses this power in mind and matter and makes them dance in their turn' (A. Coomaraswamy, *The Dance of Shiva*, Bombay : Asia Publishing House, 1948). His body being *Akash*, He dances with other four elements. The all-pervading Shakti is all delight, which is united and identified with Uma's body arising in time. The union of all time is Shiva's dance, which is 'becoming' and goes on in individual bodies as the congregation of all elements. Its deepest significance is felt when it is realized that it takes place in the heart and the self. "Everywhere is the Creator-Destroyer, everywhere is the heart", writes Coomaraswamy. He dances His cycle of grace to create all to destroy all and thus, the cycle goes on. The whole activity transubstantiates into bliss. The Supreme Intelligence dances in the human soul through the conflict of opposites to accomplish the perfect union — a vision of the self and matter in complete harmony. But He doesn't dance like a human who has a purpose, however, the reason of His dance is His own nature for His gestures are own 'nature-born' (*swabhavajaha*). Thus, Shiva's dance can be understood as the yoga (union) of the dance of nature and wisdom of soul. The dance is manifest in the universe in five activities called Panchkriyas *viz., srishti, stithi, samhar, tirobhava,* and *anugràha*; these states are defined as creation, preservation, transformation followed by new creation, diffusion of illusion, and attainment of grace or release or freedom respectively. In literary domain a parallel activity paradigm is significant — perception, fancy, imagination, intuition plus identity and consciousness.

It is these panchkriyas that become the standard of judgement. Accordingly, the poet overlooks creation and evolution, which support his wisdom to preserve Reality so he destroys and dismantles all that is unnatural. It is followed by diffusion of illusion that engulfs the mind. Confusion prevails. Further a condition descends giving rest to the same activity because only as much cosmic energy (in the form of thought) is released as can be borne by those who receive it. Thereafter is felt state of release from the restlessness of mind. It leads to attaining the grace of salvation and enjoyment of the heart — the bliss of soul. It is significant to note that having gained His purpose the poet (Shiva) ceases his cosmic activity or dance. It happened in the case of Shakespeare, Coleridge, Wordsworth, Goethe, Kabir, etc. As it is on the physical and the material plane so is it on the mental and still higher or subtler planes that Shiva (Nature) is dancing in an apparent non-system, which He alone understands. So is the instinct of the poet. "In the human form consciousness has unfolded to the highest degree so far. The human individual is a microcosm in which all the powers functions and faculties which are manifesting in the universe on a macrocosmic scale are present in a potential form or have been made partially active" (I.K. Taimini, *Hindu Symbolism*, TPH Adyar, year, p. 56). In matters of interpretation of thought character or any other phenomenon, panchkriya theory of criticism regards subjectivity portrayed objectively principles as basic. It does not negate anything. It does not begin with presumption or preconditioning of mind. It upholds the spirit of freedom in order to accept anything through reason in a state of diathesis — the most natural state of Nature itself. The process of evaluation follows rhythmic motion leading to evolution of thought and character in interrelated harmony expressing itself in spontaneous manner with a purposeless purpose to remove the snares of illusion from the mind and finally, arriving at circumstantial happiness condition and ultimately giving the feel of content (pure happiness) to one and all.

On application of this theory to Shakespeare's tragedies unconventional results are found. HAMLET and OTHELLO do not qualify as conventional tragedies, as these are according to Aristotle's POETICS or Shakespeare's own conception which define tragedy as the suffering of the good. Though the good is also restored in the end, yet it is at the cost of the good only. The evil is punished but only after it has done potential harm. In fact, both are tragedies of unreason, so are KING LEAR and MACBETH too. Unreason only breeds in evil, which is the core issue but has different reflections and shades. Conventionally, reason of evil or the cause thereof is not at all probed. The plot describes only the situation as it is. The Indian standard requires full treatment of the subject — that there is a situation, there is a cause of the same and there is also a remedy available to deal with the situation.

Now, consider HAMLET, in which intellectual activity is the whole universe and reason is the guide. Hamlet's father is dead but he didn't die a natural death. This is perception followed by fancy (*i.e. srishti* and *stithi*), so the process of discovery of truth begins with elimination of the unnatural elements through reason. The triad principle is evident. Intellectual activity (reflection) serves as *prakasa*, the substratum. It is manifest as ideas, which are played upon by vimarsa, *i.e.* by self-conscious will, knowledge and action. It is reflected in various forms and directions. Hamlet's deep thinking on identification of evil as soliloquies and interpersonal behaviour fulfils the objectives of this level. Perhaps it is the only play in which Shakespeare worked systematically and presented the core issue for thought and analysis. The cause of killing is passion or ambition. The remedy available is revenge but it poses serious questions of morality, therefore Hamlet has to work out an acceptable solution so that the real good is victorious at last. The revenge shouldn't appear as another killing rather as a punishment for doing evil. As a matter of fact Shakespeare wished that the play should be taken as a fundamental problem in itself. Shakespeare wants us to consider it a problem of humanity rather than that of Hamlet alone. The Indian standard makes further analysis. After the first two stages, a union of both follows it which is reflected as 'spand', *i.e.* as soon as Hamlet discovers unreason of his father's murder on part of Claudius, he decides to punish him. He will feel rest only when he has done so. This is what is cosmic in nature — the same principle that governs life on earth. Hamlet as an individual represents the whole universe. Nobleness of reason is Hamlet's essential character. He considers the question of evil, its nature, responsibilities of the doer and the act done. He analyses all. The whole process serves as a mirror to his mind. This is the level of samhar or imagination. He dismisses the unnatural but upholds truth. Here he is acting as per his nature without any preconditioning — (it is swabhavajaha) like Shiva. Purpose enters the mind (for he is a human being, *i.e.* limited incapacity) at the point of action. The power of distinctive self examines all aspects in a state of freedom from all affections. The power of imagination as Coleridge describes lies in its function — when it dissolves, diffuses and dissipates in order to recreate. Similar is the function of samhar. It doesn't simply destroy; rather it transforms. Hamlet comes to a condition where he is able to transcend crude subjectivity and dissolves all unreason into SUPREME REASON and the process goes on. The following lines lead to such premise :

Regarding the world : 'Fie on it! Ah fie! 'Tis an unweeded garden,/that grows to seed; things rank and gross in nature possess it merely....'

Rationality : He wants to take upon the king "in the purging of his soul". An act is worthless if 'that has no relish of salvation in it'. It implies that all fulfilment of a reasonable action is bliss. He reflects on man's state in this world : "What is man/if his chief good and market of his time/be but to sleep and feed.... Looking before and after, gave us not/that capability and god like reason/to fust in us unused...." Rightly to be great/is not to stir without great argument." So he cannot allow "excitement of (his) reason and (his) blood go to sleep." Because 'Hamlet' cannot be taken away from Hamlet himself. He can do wrong only when he is not himself. Who does it then? Obviously, his madness. He tells Leartes, "If it be so, Hamlet is of the faction that is wronged!" "His madness is poor Hamlet's enemy. Sir, in this audience, let my disclaiming from a purposed evil free me...." "The devil hath power to assume pleasing shape"/"I will have more grounds more relative than this." Thus, he wants to believe in his own reason : "To be or not to be, that is the question,/ whether 'tis nobler in the mind to suffer/the slings and arrows of outrageous fortune/or to take to arms...." "That makes calamity of so long life." Further he refers to "the oppressor's wrong or "thus conscience does make coward of us all" and "pale cast of thought" sickles "native hue of resolution".

From the above, it is possible to deduce a number of questions that are raging in his mind. *Samhar* is going on and he continues to reflect upon the core issue — How was my father killed/who killed him? Why was he killed? Should revenge be taken? Will it be justified? If killing is evil, then, is taking revenge by killing also not evil? Why should man assume responsibility to punish evil? Why not leave it to God or Nature or Supreme Intelligence? Is it necessary to think of the world in terms of good and evil? The irony of thinking is that it is not the act of revenge but the justification of the act of revenge which is the key to resolve all doubts. It is only afterwards that he will find an answer to satisfy his (but more importantly) as well as others' doubts, emotions or sentiments. No doubt, it is evil that he reflects upon. When action follows all those, who have any role in murder — remote or near, direct or indirect — are eliminated. He includes himself among the punished because he, too, commits evil by the same standard that fixes responsibility on Claudius, whether it is done to take revenge or it is anything else. Herein the working of Shakespeare's mind comes in the picture, that he makes Hamlet die though he is noble and innocent from all societal value judgements. As such the play turns out to be a real social riddle, which is very difficult to resolve. Perhaps Shakespeare intended to throw a challenge to human society, which has to be governed by double standards, which do not establish truth in any way nor build up any standard of morality, aesthetics, justice, etc. And if it is so, then why rake up the issue of truth or morality in society. In fact, creation of society itself is unjustified — it is anti-nature — then how can its premises or rules be justified on the natural principle. Shakespeare posed this serious question to human society; it's a problem; an answer has to be found, so HAMLET as a play is his ultimate reflection.

Hamlet dies a noble man and tragedy lies in the suffering of the good so by this standard HAMLET is a tragedy. But HAMLET is not a tragedy in the conventional sense simply because the hero dies in the end. Death of the hero is no justification of a tragedy. The criterion has to be found in the role of reason. It is a tragedy because, initially the good suffers, but finally reason wins and justifies the good. However, the same cannot be said about other tragedies, in which the reason of natural goodness suffers at the hands of evil but the hero never qualifies for being called the symbol of good. The folly of the conventional conception lies in the fact that it does not attach adequate significance to the element of reason of goodness. So, HAMLET is a tragedy not because the hero dies in the end but because reason of natural goodness suffers, of course temporarily; however it is established in the end. Tragedy lies in the death of a good man (Hamlet), which pains the audience, and therefore sympathy flows down to the foundation of the good. Pity has no role to play in this process for it is done to the undeserving. Moreover, the status of the goodwill stand belittled (underscored/downplayed) if it is associated with pity in any way. Similarly, going by this reason KING LEAR, MACBETH and OTHELLO are only partial tragedies whose titles are not justified; these are, in fact (may be renamed as) tragedies of Cordelia (plain truth), Duncan (trust/ambition), and Desdemona (innocence) respectively. Hamlet's essential goodness is beyond doubt. Mark the following lines :

> *Leartes* : And yet it is almost against my conscience/ exchange forgiveness with me noble Hamlet.
>
> *Hamlet* : Report me and my cause aright to the unsatisfied.
>
> *Horatio* : So cracks a noble heart.
>
> *First Ambassador* : Where should we have our thanks (pang and the sense of irreparable loss)?
>
> *Horatio* : He never gave commandment for their death.

And he mentions that deaths were caused by "Unnatural acts...put on by cunning and forced cause. And in this upshot, purposes mistook", *i.e.* to say that Hamlet lived and died like a soldier and a noble man who proved to be the most royal of all.

Thus, from all the probable questions and speeches mentioned above, it is evident that Hamlet's real problem is to reflect upon the nature of evil rather than how to take action. That's why he thinks and being a student of philosophy he has known the value of being rational so he thinks too much to justify revenge, satisfy sentiments and also make his act of revenge look non-evil, if not non-moral. Factors of delay or madness are only offshoots of such thinking. His real problem is elaborated in the famous exclamation, "What a piece of work is man! How noble in reason!" His problem is, when a man is born noble, how and why and when he turns to be ignoble and unreasonable? Horatio gives the answer in the end. Coincidentally, the world of HAMLET is a perfect representation of the cosmic scheme (dance). Accordingly, Hamlet's reason is the substratum (prakasa), which illumines all, dispels ignorance, which is an activity of will (vimarsa) to find truth and knowledge to support it. That is why 'chaitanya' of Hamlet is stimulated — an activity that is known as 'spanda' or 'sphuratta'. The desire to reflect on the nature of evil to find a rational basis of action starts-up Hamlet and he justifies himself as the protagonist of the play. On the contrary Macbeth, King Lear, and even Othello fail to do so for they suffer from a tragic flaw and nurture evil for a considerable time. Therefore, they are victims of pity more than they deserve our sympathy. The real protagonist and symbol of good in KING LEAR, Cordelia meets a tragic end. Duncan (MACBETH) is eliminated in the beginning and Othelo, the person Desdemona loves most and willingly submits to be smothered by him kills her. A serious question arises here relating to the conception of catharsis, which does not seem to hold valid. By eliminating the actual good but establishing the consolatory good, it does not really strengthen the good. We return from the theatre not with aesthetic pleasure but with a pinch of salt in the mouth. The theory of Cosmic Dance illustrates that these are partial tragedies for they do not conform to the natural principle. They represent only 'samhar' activity; *i.e.* the negative is destroyed along with the good and giving place to the good only theoretically. But what shape of good it will become is not justifiably concluded. There is also no promise for the future; the chief requirement of social morality is never fulfilled. Such literature neither adheres to nor promotes any value for it states only the situation as it is. Truly speaking, man always requires adhering to a basis of moral living or standard in order to maintain minimum social morality but the same is precariously wanting in these plays. However, the same is well illustrated in HAMLET, so it is the only perfect tragedy though not conventionally yet for the reasons stated above. Moreover, Hamlet is the only prefect tragic hero because he does not suffer from a tragic flaw unlike others. How can we regard anyone as a hero who possesses a fractured self, a stained character and an unreasonable mind? If tragedy occurs on account of hero's death, then also it is only Hamlet. The conclusion that determines evil and punishment engulfs Hamlet's too and he falls a prey to the same evil, which he wants to eradicate. In fact he is unable to resolve the million dollar question — what is moral judgement? — *vis-à-vis* his limited capability and knowledge to do justice and uphold morality. He is perhaps in search of a moral order that would be potent enough to lay down the irrevocable rules of sociomoral behaviour and the at once acceptable to all. Such order may be found only in the book of Nature, where there is always a limit to everything. Unfortunately man knows none and that is the irony of being social. As such, society is a paradox of Nature. Unless we come very close to following the laws of Nature, there can be neither certainty nor stability in sociomoral foundations. It is what Hamlet thinks upon. Mark the following : *"How weary, stale, flat, and unprofitable/Seem to me use of this world!" "Soft! Now to my mother,/O heart, lose not thy nature; let not ever/The soul of Nero enter this bosom;/Let me be cruel not unnatural"*.... *"O, this is hire and salary, not revenge."* And Hamlet's speech in Act IV Sc. Line 32 explains this aspect elaborately.

So, it is Hamlet's failure to resolve the issue adequately that recoiled on him and he has to die leading to a poignant tragedy of almost perfect class. By following his own rationale he is guilty of killing a life so his action invites punishment. Still there is grace in Hamlet's death; he is born noble and also dies a nobleman. He is not redeemed of any flaw in his character for there is none. Therefore, no catharsis takes place. Moreover, a redeemed person symbolizes only 'stained goodness'. But in HAMLET we feel satisfied because evil is vanquished. Our aesthetic sense is not fractured, nor sense of justice frustrated and we deeply mourn Hamlet's death. We rather wish that Hamlet should not have died whereas it is not so in the case of other tragic heroes. On the contrary we are not really sorry for King Lear, Othello and Macbeth. So, HAMLET is a perfect tragedy. The period of 'samhar' (imagination) is long enough in HAMLET. Tirobhava, the fourth cosmic activity, *i.e.* intuition plus identity, sets along Act II, Sc., when diffusion of illusion overtakes him. He cries in agony — a superb condemnation of his own folly — "O, what a rogue and peasant slave am I! ...to catch the conscience of the king". Now he has identified the culprit, decided and course of action that is complete in resolution. The state is short, no doubt, but it is perfect. No more moody moorings or mental engagement. With the next soliloquy when he resolves to act (II, IV...) 'Anugraha descends upon him and he moves towards attaining grace. He is resolute, firm and ready to act : "How all occasions do inform against me and spur my dull revenge/From this time forth my thought be bloody or be nothing worth." This is the level of consciousness when he understands full implications of his action especially in relation to sociomoral behaviour; he owns all those and has no grief when he has to pay a price with his life even.

The analysis explains that the third activity covers the longest span because it includes a process that has invert cycles of elimination and regeneration. The first two activities are fairly represented. But the last two being part of cycle of regression are fast and conclusive.

The merit of such holistic standard lies in evaluation of any work unto entire satisfaction and getting results free from subjective (in the narrow sense) tinge. Whereas there is due regard to the Western scholarship, the fact cannot be ignored that no standard that aims at specific conclusions and fragmentation of thought, acceptance or rejection of an idea and above all division of action or state into good and evil can lead us to satisfying conclusions. Accordingly Shakespeare's status as an artist and thinker is determined. Shakespeare is great not because he has written 'great' comedies and tragedies by any standard but because he touched the most sensitive and vital spot in our brain through the universal scheme, wherein lies the harmony of thought, emotion reason and process that gives the feeling of wholeness. An analysis of his last play, THE TEMPEST established this viewpoint. In fact Shakespeare is inspired by the 'spand' to realize the nature and extent of evil so he undergoes a process of evolution of thought from conception to fulfilment. Thereafter his mind feels satisfied. On applying Allen Tate's theory of tension, Shakespeare's in-tension is blown up to find release in ex-tension as exemplified in other tragedies. Finally his mind felt rest and did not attempt it further. He spoke only once on evil and that was all. Further, this is indisputably valid that every true poet has spoken only once, *i.e.* written only one representative work on any subject of significance.

This rule applies to all other aspects as well. It implies that as cosmic is manifest in plays so is it present in his mind too. Any development of conception does reflect evolution of thought in the mind of the playwright, which becomes the basis of theorizing. The artist experiences an impassioned vision based on understanding correlated with cloudless thinking and devoid and sentimentality. There is an evolution from knowledge to love, from illusion to transparency leading to union of inner and outer life at levels — the creator and the created. The poet or dramatist creates a universe dispassionately and gains universality through identification with Nature's law of evolution. The vision of the original poet is a discovery rather than creation (in cosmic sense) itself for he unveils beauty everywhere and recovers, however, momentarily, the unity of being released from (worldly) individuality as it is true in the case of Wordsworth. The truth is, that God or Supreme Intelligence or whatever name we give to define the Ultimate is the first creator and artist in the true sense and creation of every natural object stands as an immediate realization of His Being. The same is true in the case of literary activity. Every piece of work is a step forward in the direction of realization of artist's own ideal. Accordingly, artistic expression of character is non-volitional; no element of choice enters the world of imagination and eternity. On the contrary there is always found a perfect unity (identity) of intuition, expression, soul and body as Kabir, Shakespeare, Tagore, Aurobindo, etc. gained. As such the artist dances to the tune of Cosmic Intelligence while communicating his experience only objectively or in other words in subjectivity-abnegation-objectified manner. The two worlds of spirit and matter become one through his expression.

WORKS CITED

Capra Fritjof, *The Tao of Physics*, London, Flamingo, 1992.

The Hindu, New Delhi, 9 Jan. 2001.

SELECTED BIBLIOGRAPHY

Yogavashistha, Gita Press, Gorakhpur, 1961.

Sarva-Darshan-Sangraha of Madhavacarya. Tr. by Cowell and Gough, Parimal, Delhi, 1986.

Saundaryalhari, Sankara, Chowkhamba, Varanasi, 1950.

Patanjalyogapradeep, Gita Press, Gorakhpur, 1987.

Anand Coomraswamy, *The Dance of Shiva*, Asia Publishing House, Bombay, 1948.

K.C. Pandey, *Comparative Aesthetics Vol. I.*, Chowkhamba, Varanasi, 1959.

Ibid., Vol. II.

Ibid., Abhinavagupta, Chowkhamba, Varanasi, 1935.

Ratna Ma Navaratnam, *The Vision of Shiva in Pariapuranam*, Bhartiya Vidya Bhawan, 1987.

16

Poetry and Criticism

—K.M. Jan

Prose and Poetry

POETRY and prose are two forms of literature. They are considered antonyms but what is common to both is that both are the forms of human expression. The same words which are used in poetry are used in prose. But the level of communication achieved in poetry is different from that of prose. The words acquire a peculiar expressive power in poetry which we miss in prose. I.A. Richards in his book, *The Principles of Literary Criticism* discovered that the way we use words in prose is different from the way we use in poetry. Words in prose are used only to refer to things as they are. But in poetry words are used to produce a peculiar emotional effect. In prose words are used just to convey the sense but in poetry what matters is not the sense but the emotional impact of the language. It is just possible that the sense that the words convey in poetry runs counter to the common sense but they are capable of producing intense emotional effect. The way we use words in prose is only referential as words refer to facts or things. On the other hand the way we use words in poetry is emotive, it produces emotion in the reader. Hence, the way we use and arrange words in prose is always different from the way words are arranged in poetry, as prose conveys the sense and poetry communicates the experience adequately and powerfully. This is the basic difference between prose and poetry as the medium of communication.

Form

Mallarmé observes, "A poem is made of words, not ideas." It does not mean that ideas are incompatible with poetry. The same idea can be expressed in prose as well as poetry. Therefore the idea *per se* is not important. What makes poetry is not the idea but the form that communicates the idea. This is why the poem is always superior to its paraphrase in prose.

Form and content are inseparable. The experience comes in and through the form. The slightest alteration in form alters the experience. The form is inseparable from the content because the form is the expression of the content. Two poems on the same theme are not equivalent because their theme is the same. The form is the shape of the experience and this is what makes the real difference. This is why A.E. Houseman in his book, *The Name and Nature of Poetry*, says, "Poetry is not the thing said but a way of saying things." Therefore the words, their position and arrangement are all significant. The images, the sound, the rhythm and other elements that constitute the form impart certain qualities to the experience. The slightest alteration in the form alters the content as the experience is inherent in the shape and contour of the form.

Rhythm

Rhythm distinguishes poetry from prose. It is not that rhythm is absent from prose. While rhythm follows a regular pattern in poetry, it is irregular in prose. This leads to the natural conclusion that poetry is the rhythmical arrangement of words, in prose words are not arranged rhythmically.

Words are made of syllables. For example, the word, "begin" has two syllables — "be" and "gin". As we pronounce the word, "be" is not stressed as much as the syllable, "gin". Hence, there are two kinds of syllables — stressed or accented and unstressed or unaccented. Rhythm arises from the arrangement of stressed and unstressed syllables. It is the movement of the line. The lines in poetry move on metrical feet. Through the repetition of a particular pattern of stressed and unstressed syllables, a basic rhythmic pattern is established in poetry so that we begin to anticipate the rhythm in a line of poetry. One of the chief pleasures of poetry consists in the fulfilment of this expectation or anticipation.

Rhythm is inseparable from feeling. It is so much intimately related to feeling that it is not an exaggeration to say that every feeling has its own rhythm. Every change in rhythm reflects a change in the feeling. The dynamic rhythm reflects a spectrum of subtle shades of feeling. Poetry is not alive when the rhythm is flat, mechanical and monotonous. The change in rhythmic effects can be achieved in a variety of ways. Every stressed syllable does not carry equal weight of stress. Some syllables are heavily stressed and some are lightly stressed. A wide variety of rhythmic effects can be achieved by changing the quality of accent or stress. Alexander Pope changes the place of pause as well as the quality of stress in his poetic lines and secures a wide range of rhythmic effects, though he is strictly confined within the limits of the heroic couplet.

The relation between rhythm and feeling can be demonstrated through examples. Sometimes we listen to the wordless music on the radio. Though words are absent, this music secretly works upon our feelings. We realize that feeling has been transmitted to us through the waves of rhythm and we are in a position to state precisely the nature of the feeling communicated to us through the rhythm or the wordless music, whether the feeling is light-hearted or sad. Wordsworth's poem "The Solitary Reaper" communicates a similar experience. Wordsworth did not know the Scottish language, but he was moved by the rhythm of the Scottish song of the solitary repear. The pathos of the song was communicated to the poet through the rhythm or the rise and fall of the voice despite the fact that the language was unknown to the poet. Thus rhythm is able to transmit the feeling without intelligible or tangible words. T.S. Eliot was referring to the same fact when he remarked that "Genuine poetry can communicate before it is understood." Every genuine poetry is charged with the special power of rhythm. When rhythm cooperates with the sense or feeling, the expression is powerful :

> How to keep to keep — is there any, is there none such,
> nowhere known some, how or brooch or braid or brace,
> lace, latch or catch or key to keep.
> Back beauty, keep it, beauty, beauty, beauty,... from
> vanishing away?
>
> (The Leaden Echo and the Golden Echo)

Here the rhythm of the lines communicates the restless anxiety of the speaker to keep beauty from vanishing away. Almost all the words are monosyllabic creasing the impression of a very swift movement. The alternatives are joined by the conjunction "or" in the beginning of the line but soon it disappears altogether to further accelerate the rhythm of the line. The hurrying rhythm of the line which gathers momentum reflects the rising restless anxiety of the speaker. But the rising rhythm of the line almost stops at the word "back" suggesting almost a physical effort at holding back, the last effort exerted by the speaker and then the check of the rhythm is released suggesting the utter helpless of the poet with the loss of the tight physical hold as he sees the beauty actually vanishing away.

In William Shakespeare's play, *Macbeth* the following lines are remarkable :

> The light thickens and the crow
> Makes wing to rooky woods.

Our voice stops with the word, "crow" in the first line and the two equally accented syllables ("makes", "wings") in the first part of the second line suggest the fast movement that the crow makes to reach the rooky wood. A very fine example of how the rhythm enacts the meaning is available in John Keats's poem, "Ode to Autumn" :

> And sometimes like a gleaner thou dost keep
> Steady thy laden head across a brook.

Here the first line is in iambic producing the impression of a regular movement. But the first foot of the second line is stressed which interrupts the regular iambic movement and reflects the balancing movement of the gleaner.

It is obvious from the above examples that rhythm is the essential part of the poetic meaning. It can suggest actions, physical movements and communicate states of mind and feeling to the reader. Poetry becomes a living experience for the reader on account of the suggestive power of the rhythm which is one with the sense and feeling.

Imagery

The experience of poetry is not only the experience of rhythm. It is also the experience of imagery. In the heightened emotional state, the poet's mind is unusually sensitive. He is able to relate his emotional experiences to objects and phenomena in the outside world. His emotional experiences are defined through such images. The abstract experience becomes concrete through imagery and the emotion acquires a condensed form of expression. If the images is banal, trite and hackneyed, it is likely to make no immediate impact on the reader like the old, rubbed-out coins which do not catch our attention. But when the image is the result of fresh perception and is striking, it has the immediacy of effect as in Dylan Thomas's poem, "Fern Hill":

> I was happy as the grass was green.

The feeling of happiness is projected through the image of "green grass". The comparison of happiness to "green grass" is immediately striking because it is the result of fresh perception. The subjective feeling of the poet has acquired a concrete sensuous form through the image of "green grass". As the poet cannot transfer his feelings directly to the reader, it is through the imagery that he is able to communicate his feelings in the concentrated form.

Imagery has been the staple vehicle of poetic meaning since times immemorial, but it has received greater critical attention during the imagist movement in the thirties. The evocative power comes to poetry through visual, auditory, olfactory, tactile and kinetic imagery. Keats's poetry is rich in sensuous imagery.

Romantic poetry contains images which are remarkable for sensuous beauty. But in metaphysical poetry the character of imagery is intellectual. It is the essential part of the meaning. It does not attract attention for its individual splendour. Sometimes the images are completely without any special power to attract but they are essential for the communication of the peptic meaning, for example,

> The day lingered on
> Like an unwanted guest.

"The unwanted guest" is not a beautiful image, but it is necessary to express the feeling of ennui or sense of boredom. Andrew Marvell's poem, "The Definition of Love" contains, not decorative but functional images of oblique and parallel lines :

> As lines so loves oblique
> May themselves in every corner greet
> But ours so truly parallel, though infinite
> Can never meet.

Here the images of geometry have tremendous power to suggest the definitions of the finite and infinite loves. The poet uses the word, "corner", instead of "angle" as the sense of secrecy of clandestine love is suggested by the image of corner rather than the image of angle. Similarly parallel lines which form no angle or corner and which never meet contain the definition of infinite love. Henry Vaughan in his poem, "The Retreat", makes a beautiful use of colour imagery. The colour, "white" is associated with the light of the purity of childhood. The colour "white", is replaced by the colour, "black" in the poem as childhood is replaced by adulthood and the man learns the "black art" of living in the world. Thus the poem suggests through the interplay of colours the journey of man from the brilliant purity of childhood to the black adulthood which is contaminated with sin.

Imagery imparts the evocative and suggestive power to poetry. Through the analysis of images and their patterns we can discern the deeper meanings of poetry as in the poetic tragedies of William Shakespeare. There is vivid realization of experience in words in terms of imagery and the abstract subjective experiences acquire a palpable form. Yet there is much poetry which is described as the poetry of statement. It contains little imagery yet it is charged with great emotional power.

Sound

Sound plays an important role in poetry. It is not that the poet always deliberately creates these sound effects. As sounds are part of the language, they render the experience more palpable and concrete. Many of the rhetorical devices are, in fact, nothing but the arrangement of particular sound effects in the language. They contribute to the poetic effect as the experience is immediately communicated to the reader. The most obvious form of the participation of the sound in the meaning is onomatopoeia. The oft-quoted line of Tennyson "the humming of innumerable bees" is an example of onomatopoeia where the predominance of the nasal sounds (m, n) in "humming" and "innumerable" produces the noise actually made by the bees.

Apart from onomatopoeia, alliteration is a source of music in poetry, in Wordsworth's poem, "A slumber did my spirit seal". Quite appropriately, the poem begins the charming effect of sibilant sounds and achieves the soft, gentle effect of dreaminess in the poem. In the line of Shakespeare, "How sweet the moonlight sleeps upon this bank", the beautiful effect is produced by the combination of alliteration and personification. The charm of the moonlit night on the riverside is communicated to us through the mellifluous music of repeated sibilant sounds as well as the personification of the moonlight in the line. The beautiful effect of the lines of Andrew Marvel's poem, "To His Coy Mistress" depends on sound effect :

But at my back I always hear
Time's winged chariot hurrying near

In the first half of the first line "b" sound strikes against "t" sound, "d" sound against "t" and "b" against "k" sound respectively recreating the sound produced by the hoof of the chariot horses. In the second half of the line these sounds are absent. Thus the sounds of the line enact the sense of the line where the sound of the chariot of time is audible at the back or the first half of the line only.

Thomas Hardy's poem "A Broken Appointment" is able to achieve a rare fusion of sound and sense.

You did not come
And marching time drew on, and wore me numb —
Yet less for loss of your dear presence there
Than that I thus found lacking in your make
That high compassion which can overbear
Reluctance for pure loving kindness sake
Grieved I, when, as the hope-hour stroked its sum.
You did not come.

You love not me
And love alone can lend you loyalty
— I know and knew it. But unto the store
of human deeds divine in all but name, —
Was it not worth a little hour or more
To add yet this : once you, a woman came
To soothe a time-torn man, even though it be
You love not me.

The sound is important in this poem in the form of rhyme. The first stanza contains the rhymes, "come", "numb", "sum" and "come" which produce a chiming effect. The mind of the lover is preoccupied with the passage of time as he is waiting for the arrival of his beloved. Quite naturally the rhymes which occur in the first stanza project the time-obsessed consciousness of the lover. As waiting gives way to despair, the chiming rhymes of the first stanza give way to another set of rhymes, "me", "loyalty", "be" and "me" which do not sound like the striking of the clock. Thus waiting for the appointed time of the beloved's arrival is communicated powerfully through the rhymes.

In Lord Tennyson's poem, "The Brook", the poetic lines have a memorable quality of sound and rhythm. The sound and rhythm are fused and fused together with the sense. We hear different sounds of the brook on rocks and plain :

I chatter overstay ways
    In little sharps and trebles

I bubble into eddying bays
    I babble on the pebbles.

The sounds made by "chatter", "sharps", "trebles", "bubble", "babble", "eddying bays" and "pebbles" recreate in our imagination the stream of water gushing through hard rocks and pebbles. On the other hand, the gentle flow of the brook on the plain is reflected in a different kind of sounds in the line :

Till last by Philip's farm I flow
    To join the brimming river
For men may come and men may go
    But I go on for ever.

The "soft" "f" sound which recurs again and again in "Philip", "farm" and "flow" creates the sweet flowing rhythm and sound of the brook which joins "the brimming river". The repetition of "m" and "r" sounds in "brimming river" further heightens the impression of the sweet flowing music of the brook on the river and on the plain.

Four Kinds of Meaning

I.A. Richards in his book, *Practical Criticism* has found four kinds of meaning or four aspects of meaning : sense, feeling, tone and intention. As understanding of the communication is the first task that any reader is faced with, the classification of four aspects of meaning is a useful tool for the analysis and understanding of any form of communication.

1. Sense. We speak to say something, we direct the attention of the hearer to some state of affairs or present some items for consideration, it is described as sense by Richards.

2. Feeling. When we say something, we have usually some feeling for the state of affairs or the items at the same time. We use language to express this feeling or nuance of interest and it is the essential part of the meaning.

3. Tone. When the speaker speaks, he has an attitude to his listener. As the audience varies, the tone of utterance also changes which reflects a changing relationship with the audience. He chooses and arranges his words differently with each set of audience.

4. Apart from sense, feeling and tone, intention is a very important aspect of meaning. Through sense, feeling and tone, the speaker, consciously or consciously aims to promote an effect. To understand the intention of the speaker is part of the business of apprehending meaning.

These tools are useful in analyzing the language of communication. Failure of our part to understand any of these functions may grossly distort the sense, feeling tone and intention resulting in the failure of comprehension.

Trends in English Poetry

So far we have considered how several elements of words are used in poetry. We need to take into account more than sound, rhythm, and imagery. The nature and character of poetry is determined by the ways in which these elements of words are used by the poets. Shakespeare, Herbert, Pope, Eliot and Yeats use words differently from the way Spenser, Milton, Tennyson and Swinburn do.

While Spenser, Milton and Tennyson exploit the musical properties of the language, the poets in the Shakespearian-Donne tradition do not exploit the musical properties of the language so much as use the rhythm of common speech in their poetry. It account for a world of difference between two kinds of poetry. While Spenser, Milton and Tennyson exhibit a feeling for words, Shakespeare and Donne feel through words. The music of words dominates the poetry of Spenserian tradition whereas there is the music of meaning in the Shakespearean tradition. While Spenserian poetry is descriptive, Shakespearean poetry is dramatic. Beautiful passages of description are available in the Spenserian tradition as in Shelley's "To a Skylark" :

Like a high-born maiden
In a palace tower
Soothing her love-laden

Soul in secret hour
With music sweet as love, which overflows her bower.

But the living human voice is missing. When poetry is dramatic, the human voice is audible in the rhythm of the line :

If it were done, when it is done, then 'twere well
It were done quickly;

or

For God's sake hold your tongue and let me love

We get a very vivid presentation of the situation in which the speaker is compelled to express himself. There is immediacy of effect as we are directly in contact with a concrete human situation and the urgency of feeling is reflected in the speech rhythm and the dramatic tone. The poetic experience is a living experience with the urgent tone of voice, speech rhythm and concrete human situation. This poetry is definitely different from the descriptive poetry of the Spenserian tradition.

Practical Criticism

Sir Ifor Evans remarks, "Literature helps us to understand life and criticism helps us to understand literature." Eliot thinks that the aim of criticism is to enhance our understanding and enjoyment of poetry (literature). The critic analyses his impressions of a poem. He examines the poem in its different parts with the understanding that a poem is more than its parts because it includes the relation between the parts. There are two sides of criticism : theory and practice. The criticism that deals with the principles of literature is called theoretical criticism. The criticism which applies these theories to the works of art is practical criticism. It directly deals with work of art or poem.

The impressions of the critic are not arbitrary or whimsical but are based on and related to the facts of the poem. We can confirm the impressions of the critic by comparing his impressions with the facts of the poem by going through it. A critic is a sensitive reader who is unusually perceptive. He can discover the beauties that other readers might have missed. He does not pass judgement but makes us see what we have failed to perceive. In this way, criticism enhances our understanding and enjoyment of poetry.

TO THE VIRGINS, TO MAKE MUCH OF TIME

Gather ye Rose buds, while ye May,
Old Time is still a-flying :
And this same flower that smiles today
Tomorrow will be dying.

The glorious Lamp of Heaven, the Sun,
The higher he's a getting;
The sooner will his Race be run,
And nearer he's to setting.

The Age is best which is the first,
When Youth and Blood are warmer;
But being spent, the worse, and worst
Times, still succeed the former.

Then be not coy, but use your time;
And while ye may, go marry;
For having lost but once your prime,
You may for ever tarry.

—Robert Herrick

Robert Herrick's favourite theme is *carpe diem*. In poem after poem, he gives expression to the feeling that time flies away and with it all that we love, all that we care for. Shakespeare grants immortality to his young friend's beauty by focusing on it in the immortal work of his art. But no such idea is there to console Robert Herrick.

The first stanza of the poem contains the images of rosebuds, smiling flower, dying flower, today and tomorrow. The "old time" has been qualified with the phrase, "a-flying". The effect of the flying time is illustrated in the speed with which changes occur with the passage of time, from today to tomorrow — the smiling flower changes into the dying flower. The suggested idea is that rosebuds will not last beyond today. Hence, the advice of the poet, "Gather ye rosebuds while ye May." The rosebuds stand for the pleasures or the joys of life which are to vanish into the thin air. The rosebuds are also the virgins who will not stay youthful and beautiful as today.

The universal law of decay which is embodied in the rosebuds is illustrated by the natural images of the sun also. The rising sun turns into the setting sun within the short span of a day. It is remarkable that the line, "The higher he is a getting rhymes with the line", "And nearer he's to setting" suggesting that getting higher and setting are part of the rhythm of time in which the race of the sun is run. Youth and age present the same facet of reality that growth and decay are part of the same rhythm of time. The speed of growth is the speed of decay. The warmth of youth and blood is spent with time. While youth is "best", the age is "worst". The universal principle of nature is inherent in all these images.

The last stanza of the poem is didactic. In the light of the images of decay that nature presents, the poet urges girls to "use your time" and "go marry". Though there is a direct address to the girls, a close scrutiny of the poem reveals that it is not a poem on girls so much as on the effect of time. It brings to light the fact that even beauty is no guarantee against the inexorable law of time — decay. The poem paints the universal picture of decay, the evanescence of beauty and then gives expression to the natural impulse to seize the passing moment before it vanished away. It is a light, lovely lyric on the evanescence of beauty and the passage of time, the favourite theme of Robert Herrick.

BLUE GIRLS

Twirling your blue skirts, travelling the sward
Under the towers of your seminary,
Go listen to your teachers old and contrary
Without believing a word.

Tie the white fillets then about your hair
And think no more of what will come to pass
Than bluebirds that go walking on the grass
And chattering on the air.

Practise your beauty, blue girls, before it fail,
And I will cry with my loud lips and publish
Beauty which all our power shall never establish,
It is so frail.

For I could tell you a story which is true
I know a lady with a terrible tongue,
Blear eyes fallen from blue,
All her perfections tarnished — yet it is not long
Since she was lovelier than any of you

—John Crowe Ransom

John Crowe Ransom's poem, "Blue Girls" is the modern version of Robert Herrick's theme of *carpe diem*. The poem has certainly the echoes of Robert Herrick's poem, "Gather ye Rosebuds" as it immediately reminds of Herrick's poem. In spite of close resemblance, the poem has a life of its own, a charm of its own. Herrick's poem contains images of nature like bud, flower, sun, to suggest decay as the inescapable law of nature and in the light of these images of nature urges the girls to make most of their time.

Ransom's poem, "Blue Girls" has a slightly different patterns. The first stanza of the poem presents the images of intellectual pursuit, seminary and teachers, but also qualifies them with adjectives, "teachers old and contrary" with a direction to the blue girls to listen to their teachers "without believing a word". There is a sharp contrast between "towers of seminary", "teachers old and contrary" and "grass" and "chattering on the air". The first set of images is associated with intellectual pursuit and the second set consists of natural, instinctive things. The "bluebirds" are set against "teachers old and contrary". The blue birds are neither old nor contrary as they follow no intellectual pursuits but their instincts. It is remarkable that the adjective "blue" qualifies both "skirts" and "girls" indicating something common between them ("girls" and "eyes" are also blue in the poem). One feature of the "bluebirds" is that they "think no more of what will come to pass", "go walking on the grass" and "chattering on the air". The poet urges the blue girls to act in the manners of bluebirds — to avoid intellection which is represented by "seminary" and "teachers", to follow the ways of the birds as they are also "blue" like birds. The eyes were also "blue". But from "blue" they have turned "blear". The last stanza states that when the lady was "lovelier than any of you", her eyes were "blue". When all her perfections are "tarnished", her eyes have turned "blear". In the context of the poem, the adjective, "blue" comes to suggest youthful beauty. The greatest achievement of Ransom is that he has been able to impart a new meaning to the adjective, "blue". The word is reborn with a new meaning in the poem.

The poem, on the one hand, sets up a parallel between bluebirds and blue girls and, on the other hand, sets the example of a lady with "a terrible tongue" and "blue eyes" which could not retain their blueness through the passage of time. In this background, the poet urges blue girls to "practise your beauty before it fail".

Herrick's poem, instead of setting the example of the lady, illustrates the law of nature in the decay of flowers, the sun, and youth and urges girls not to be coy but "use your time". Ransom's poem follows almost a similar pattern as Herrick's. Herrick's poem employs only one kind of imagery, of natural things, but the imagery of Ransom's poem involves the principle of contrast in the poem. There is fresh imagery as well as a complex relationship between the images in the poem of Ransom. There is also a greater creative ability at work as the word "blue" is recreated in the context with a new meaning.

THE RETREAT

Happy those early days, when I
Shined in my Angel-infancy!
Before I understood this place
Appointed for my second race,
Or taught my soul to fancy aught
But a white, celestial thought;
When yet I had not walk'd above
A mile or two from my first Love,

And looking back, at the short space
Could see a glimpse of His bright face;
When on some gilded cloud or flower
My gazing soul would dwell an hour,
And in those weaker glories spy
Some shadows of eternity;
Before I taught my tongue to wound
My conscience with a sinful sound,
Or had the black art to dispense
A several sin to every sense,
But felt through all this fleshy dress
Bright shoots of everlastingness.

O how I long to travel back,
And tread again that ancient track!
That I once more might reach that plain,
Where first I left my glorious train;
From whence th'enlighten'd spirit sees
That shady city of Palm-trees!
But ah! my soul with too much stay
Is drunk, staggers in the way —
Some men a forward motion love,
But I by backward steps would move;
And when this dust falls to the urn,
In that state I came, return.

—Henry Vaughan

Henry Vaughan is a metaphysical poet. He has the temperament of a mystic poet. He writes of nature and childhood as Wordsworth would write. His soul is ever questing back to the days of his own youth or to the youth of the world when God and man were in more intimate contact. "The Retreat" is a nostalgic poem which represents Vaughan at his best.

The poem expresses Vaughan's earnest longing "to travel back" to his angel infancy, to the happy early days before he understood this world. It deals with the journey of man from his infancy rather from the expulsion of man from the garden of Eden to his return to dust. The poem is built on a contrast between the early days of angel-infancy and adulthood. The journey in time or ageing implies travelling away from God, and the natural brightness which characterizes childhood. The colour imagery becomes prominent in the contrast. Infancy is associated with the white colour and adulthood with black. The thought in infancy is "white" and "celestial". At the same time infancy is associated with light which is present in words like "shined", "angel", "gilded", "glory", "bright face" and "bright shoots of everlastingness". As infancy gives way to adulthood, the white colour is replaced by the black colour. Adulthood is associated with "black art", "sinful tongue" and "wounded conscience". Innocence, the light of the purity of the soul is lost as it learns the black art of living in this world.

The images of "walk a mile or two", "looking back" suggest the journey of the forward motion. The second stanza presents the image of retreat with its "travel back", "ancient track", "tread again" and "reach that plain". The second stanza expresses the longing of the poet to regain his whiteness or the glory of the soul. The longing is powerfully communicated with rhymes stressing "back", "track", "plain", "train", "sees" and "trees". "The Shady City of Palm Trees", suggests the lost garden of Eden which the poet wants to regain by his backward steps when his dust falls to the urn.

Vaughan has stylistic affiliations with Marvell. While Marvell uses the image "green thought", Vaughan uses the image of "white celestial thought". Wordsworth uses the phrase "celestial light" in his poem, "Ode on the Intimations of Immortality" which runs parallel to "The Retreat" in theme. A significant difference between the poem of Vaughan and that of Wordsworth is that though both the poets lament the loss of "a white, celestial thought" or "celestial light", the God whose nearness the poet describes is much more present in Vaughan's poem than in Wordsworth's. Wordsworth "is readier to rest in nature than the God of nature." The poem, "The Retreat" registers the mystical temper of Vaughan. His religious sensibility distinguishes him from Wordsworth, though he exhibits a similar feelings for nature or childhood.

O MY LUVE'S LIKE A RED, RED ROSE

O My Luve's like a red, red rose
That's newly sprung in June :
O my Luve's like the melodie
That's sweetly play'd in tune.

As fair art thou, my bonnie lass,
So deep in luve am I :

And I will luve thee still, my dear,
Till a' the seas gang dry:

Till a' the seas gang dry, my dear,
And the rocks melt wi' the sun;
I will luve thee still, my dear,
While the sands o' life shall run.

—Robert Burns

Robert Burns is an eighteenth century poet who is one of the precursors of the romantic revival. The romantic spontaneous overflow of powerful feelings is something that distinguishes this poem from the Augustan tradition and links it with the romantic. The occasion of the poem is the temporary separation of the poet from his beloved. The entire poem takes the form of assurance from the lover to the beloved that his emotion of love is strong enough to bring him back to her.

The poem brings with a simile, "O my luve's like a red, red rose". The repetition of the adjective, "red" gives the impression of an intensely red rose which is the symbol of the poet's love for his beloved. The comparison between the poet's love and the "red, red rose" suggests that his love is fresh like an intensely red rose which is newly sprung in June. Hence, it is not going to fade soon. The poet further compares his love to melody which reflects the pleasant sweetness of this emotion. The poem also puts emphasis on the desirability of his "fair" and "bonnie" beloved and his equally deep love.

The hyperboles in the poem reinforce the impression of the undying love of the poet for his beloved :

And I will luve thee still, my dear,
Till a' the seas gang dry :
Till a' the seas gang dry, my dear,
And the rocks melt wi' the sun;

The hyperboles state that it is possible for the seas to dry up and the rocks to melt in the sun, but it is not possible that the sea of his love for the beloved will dry up. The auxiliary "will" in place of "shall" with the personal pronoun, "I" suggests the emotional force behind the poet's promise to continue to love to the end of his life. The same auxiliary is present in "And I will luve thee stil, my dear/while the sands o' life shall run." It is the last arrow in the armoury of the poet to kill the doubt in the mind of the beloved about the genuineness of his love.

The poem has all the virtues of a fine lyric. Almost all the words of the poem are monosyllabic. It results in the fast rhythmical movement of the line. Moreover, the alliteration of "r" and "l" in "O my luve's like a red, red rose", the repetition of words like "red", the phrases, "my dear", "my luve" and the lines, "Till a' the seas gang dry" and "I will luve thee still, my dear" lends a rich musicality to the poem. The fast rhythm, the music and the hyperboles in the poem form an appropriate vehicle for the expression of a strong, spontaneous feeling of the poet's love for his beloved. The poem is highly successful as a lyric as it communicates powerfully the intensity of the poet's personal feeling.

STOPPING BY WOODS ON A SNOWY EVENING

Whose woods are these are I think I know.
His house is in the village though;
He will not see me stopping here
To watch his woods fill up with snow.

My little horse must think it queer
To stop without a farmhouse near
Between the woods and frozen lake
The darkest evening of the year.

He gives his harness bell a shake
To ask if there is one mistake
The only other'sound's the sweep
Of easy wind and downy flake.

The woods are lovely dark and deep.
But I have promises to keep,
And miles to go before I sleep,
And miles to go before I sleep.

—Robert Frost

Robert Frost is a modern American poet. He stands at the confluence of the nineteenth and the twentieth century. He blends the anecdotal method of Wordsworth with the symbolic technique of the modernists. The poem, "Stopping by Woods on a Snowy Evening" is a case in point.

The poem presents a scene. The poet in his journey on a horseback "stops to watch" "the woods fill up with snow" the woods which "are lovely, dark and deep". They are so lovely, that on the darkest evening of the year, he has stopped between the woods and the frozen lake, though there is no farmhouse in the neighbourhood. There is perfect silence all around except the bell of the horse and "the only sound's the sweep of easy wind and downy flake". It is unusual for the poet as well as his horse to stop in this way in the middle of the journey. The horse, therefore, gives his harness bells a shake to ask his master if he has committed a mistake. The poet in unable to stop here to enjoy the momentary break in his journey, because he has to keep his promises "and miles to go before I sleep." The repetition of the line, "And miles to go before I sleep" suggests the long, monotonous and tiring nature of the journey he has to undertake.

The poem yields interpretations at several levels. Literally, the poem presents a moment in the life of a horseman on his way. The success of the poet lies in the precise evocation of the scene. The way the details of the scene been selected and arranged in the poem suggests symbolic meanings as well.

The journey has been a traditional Christian symbol of life in this world as we find in John Bunyan's *Pilgrim's Progress*. Viewed from this angle, "the lovely, dark and deep woods" are worldly attractions along the path of life which allure us away from the Christian discipline of life. The man is attracted to them but refuses to succumb to them and goes on to follow the tiring, monotonous path of life. Though the poem gives an allegorical meaning, it remains a living vignette from the rural life of New England.

The poem is pregnant with rich, symbolic meanings. In the backdrop of the tiring monotony of life, the lovely, dark and deep woods which attract the poet and make him stop on his way represent death. The poet's desire to stop is the expression of this desire to opt out of the tiring journey of life. But he has in mind the commitments of life which he cannot give up in spite of his desire to do so. He cannot "sleep" before he has gone miles and miles on the same path. "Sleep" suggests stoppage of activity or death.

Robert Frost's poems are symbolic and the point of the poem is generally stated explicitly as in "Mending Wall" or "Two Tramps at Mudtime". But "Stopping by Woods on a Snowy Evening" does not state the point explicitly. The image suggests the idea as there is perfect fusion between the idea and the image.

UPON WESTMINSTER BRIDGE

Earth has not anything to show more fair :
Dull would he be of soul who could pass by
A sight so touching in its majesty :
This City now both like a garment wear
The beauty of the morning : silent, bare,
Ships, towers, domes, theatres, and temples lie
Open unto the fields, and to the sky,
All bright and glittering in the smokeless air

Never did sun more beautifully steep
In his first splendour valley, rock, or hill;
Ne'er saw I, never felt, a calm so deep;

The river glideth at his own sweet will;
Dear God! the very houses seem asleep;
And all that mighty heart is lying still!

—William Wordsworth

Wordsworth is the pioneer of the Romantic movement in English poetry. Nature in his poetry is not the object of romantic passion but of religious devotion. He reveals an attitude of mystical pantheism towards nature in his poetry. He is specially sensitive to the calm of the evening and morning. This is why Wordsworth presents the beautiful calm of the city of London in the morning hour in "Upon Westminster Bridge".

"Upon Westminster Bridge" is a sonnet. It presents the panoramic view of London from Westminster Bridge. The morning scene of London is arresting in its beauty and unearthly in its splendour. The personification of the city in the line, "The City now both like a garment wear/The beauty of the morning" is the poem in brief. The rest of the poem is only the detail of the morning garment. The simile and the personification in the line suggest that the beauty of the morning is only the garment of the city. It will be cast off as the city changes its dress. The morning garment is composed of "silent, bare ships, towers, domes, theatres and temples" "open unto the fields and to the sky". The city of London is silent, bare, bright and gliterring in the smokeless air of the morning. The perfect calm of the city is something unknown to Londoners. The unusually bright and still panorama of the city catches the attention of the poet and he is so much affected by a "sight so touching in its majesty" that he exclaims that "earth has not anything to show more fair" and only a person, dull of soul can ignore it.

Personification is the staple vehicle of expression in the poem. The personification of the city that wears the morning beauty like a garment remains the central image in the poem. The sun which beautifully steeps in "his first splendour" valley, rock and hill and the river that glides "at his own sweet will" are personified. The bridge presents a calm, bright panorama of London. The impression of brilliance as well as perfect silence that envelops the city is made by the frequent use of words like "silent", "a calm so deep", "asleep" and "still". The personification of the houses which "seem asleep" makes the impression of perfect silence and complete absence of activity. "Mighty heart" is a metaphor for London which suggests the pounding noise of the traffic and factories. What makes the poet wonder is that the throbbing city of London is still. London is here associated with unusually clear brightness and silence and somnolescence in the morning, a garment that the city usually does not put on for the day. It attracts the poet and the poem is a record of his response to this breathtaking scene.

Romantic poetry is descriptive by nature and Wordsworth is at the height of his descriptive powers in this poem. To Wordsworth "Poetry is the spontaneous overflow of powerful feelings recollected in tranquillity." The recollection recreates the scene for the reader with all its precise details, atmosphere at the sensation and feelings that attend upon it. Wordsworth's poetry is not the poetry of effusion like Shelley. He is able to recreate the objective correlative by selecting the relevant details of a scene in his poetry. "Upon Westminster Bridge" is a Petrarchan sonnet with a slight difference in the rhyme-scheme which runs as abba, abba, cde, dcd. It shows that not only Shakespeare and Milton are the masters of the sonnet. One important in this field is William Wordsworth.

IN TIME OF "THE BREAKING OF NATIONS"

Only a man harrowing clods
    In a slow silent walk
With an old horse that stumbles and nods
    Half asleep as they stalk.

Only thin smoke without flame
    From the heaps of couch-grass;
Yet this will go onward the same
    Though Dynasties pass.

Yonder a maid and her wight
    Come whispering by :

War's annals will cloud into night
Ere their story die.

—Thomas Hardy

Thomas Hardy is a great novelist and poet of our own age. He expresses his tragic vision of life in his novels. His poetry is the direct expression of his experiences. His poems start immediately out of his own remembered past and are particular evocations of utter loss, blindness of chance and poignancy of love against the cruelty of time.

The poem, "In Time of 'The Breaking of Nations' " was written after the outbreak of the First World War. The poem presents the background of the war. Against this background, his vision of the eternal and permanent is projected. The poet works through the juxtaposition of images. The first presents the image of a man with an old horse. The horse stumbles and nods as he is harrowing clods in a slow, silent walk. The image is associated with ploughing, sowing and harvesting, the permanent recurring events in nature. The second stanza extends the idea of the first as it presents the brilliance of the couch-grass, a symbol of growth in nature. The poet suggests, as Tennyson does in "The Brook", that the scenes in nature are eternal. They will remain the same, though the dynasties pass off.

Third and the last stanza which concludes the poem grows out of the preceding ones. This stanza presents an image. A girl and her loves are going by, whispering to each other. This scene like the previous one from nature represents the eternal. The dynasties and the history of wars are ephemeral. But the passion of love and love-making is an eternal process of life.

It is a modern poem as it works through images, symbols and juxtapositions. Hardy is more modern in his poetry than in his novels as far as the presentment is concerned.

SAILING TO BYZANTIUM

I

That is no country for old men. The young
In one another's arms, birds in the trees

— Those dying generations — at their song,
The salmon-falls, mackerel-crowded seas,
Fish, flesh, or fowl commend all summer long
Whatever is begotten, born, and dies.
Caught in that sensual music all neglect
Monuments of unageing intellect.

II

An aged man is but a paltry thing,
A tattered coat upon a stick, unless
Soul clap its hands and sings, and louder sing
For every tatter in its mortal dress,
Nor is there singing school but studying
Monuments of its own magnificence;
And therefore I have sailed the seas and come
To the holy city of Byzantium.

III

O sages standing in God's holy fire
As in the gold mosaic of a wall,
Come from the holy fire, perinea in a gyre,
And be the singing-masters of my soul.
Consume my heart away; sick with desire
And fastened to a dying animal
It knows not what it is; and gather me
Into the artifice of eternity.

IV

Once out of nature I shall never take
My bodily form from any natural thing,
But such a form as Grecian goldsmiths make
Of hammered gold and gold enamelling
To keep a drowsy Emperor awake;
Or set upon a golden bough to sing
To lords and ladies of Byzantium
Of what is past, or passing, or to come.

—W.B. Yeats

W.B. Yeats stands out as great poet of the first half of the twentieth century. His poetry is remarkable not for the mystery, the magic or even the atmosphere that one finds in his poetry but the passion, the humanity, the technical perfection and the strength and vitality of his response.

Yeats has written two poems on Byzantium. The poem "Sailing to Byzantium" grapples with the personal conflict of the poet, the problem of ageing. Yeats transmutes the personal experience into something rich strange, something universal and impersonal. The poem, "Sailing to Byzantium" has this beauty. The poet says, "I have sailed the seas and come to the holy city of Byzantium but this is the journey of every man from the strength of body to the maturity of the mind. As the title of the poem suggests, it is about the poet's sailing from Ireland to Byzantium. On the symbolic plane it is a transition from sensual art to intellectual art, from the body to the mind, from process to perfection. The first stanza celebrates the "sensual music" of "flesh, fish or fowl" which finds concrete form in "the young in one another's arms" and "birds in the trees at their song". The salmon-falls and the mackerel-crowded seas form part of the music. Here "caught" is the key-word. Man is caught in that sensual music as in a net. The "monument of unageing intellect" might be verse or any artistic creation to which the young are completely indifferent. This is the picture of Ireland which "is no country for old men". Ireland, thus, emerges as a symbol of youthful energy and vitality. It expresses the poet's nostalgia for the strength and the vitality of the young.

The second stanza in contrast with the first is not "about the sensual music of the young in one another's arm", but the aged man, not Ireland but Byzantium. In contrast with the young, the aged man is a paltry thing", "a tattered coat upon a stick", the reverse of what once he was. It suggests the poet's deeply felt sense of loss at the passing of the splendour and glory of the youth. The old have their mind. They are "fastened to a dying animal". But the mind can be yet supreme. The poet's nostalgia is tempered by his acceptance of age with its compensations in poetic achievement or intellectual powers.

The irony of the youthful, glowing body is that it is "a dying animal". Therefore the poet appeals to sages to consume his heart and to transform him to "a bodily form" which is not taken from any natural thing. As the myth goes, in the Emperor's palace at Byzantium was a tree of gold and silver and artificial birds sang to lords and ladies. It is what the poet calls "the artifice of eternity". The poet prefers "the artifice of eternity" to the natural thing as it is subject to the processes of change through time or "past", present and future. The golden birds of Byzantium sing of "what is past, passing or to come" echoing the rhythm of "Whatever is begotten, born or dies" in the first stanza. Eliot catches the rhythm of natural life in "birth, copulation and death". "The birds in the trees at their song" in the first stanza is contextually connected with "dying generations". It ironically echoes Keats's "Ode to a Nightingale" where the nightingale is an immortal bird. Like "Ode to a Nightingale", it contrasts process with perfection, transience with eternity, the sensual with the intellectual, the natural, with the mythical.

The poem, "Sailing to Byzantium" is built on a series of contrasts between the "sensual music" and the "monument of unageing intellect", "dying generations" and "artifice of eternity, natural and mythical, Ireland and Byzantium". The complex richness of the poem derives from the dynamic tension that holds together the opposed sets of images.

LOVE'S PHILOSOPHY

The fountains mingle with the river
And the river with the ocean,
The winds of heaven mix for ever
With a sweet emotion;
Nothing in the world is single,
All things by law divine
In one another's being mingle —
Why not I with thine?

See the mountains kiss high heaven
And the waves clasp one another;
No sister flower will be forgiven
If it disdain'd its brother;
And the sunlight clasps the earth,

And the moonbeams kiss the sea —
What are all these kissing worth,
If thou kiss not me?

—P.B. Shelley

"Love's Philosophy" is a lyric. It is a love poem, an invitation to the beloved to fall in with the universal law of nature and to "mingle" with the poet through a gesture of love. The poem consists of two stanzas. Both have a cyclic repetitive form. The first stanza presents the images of nature — fountains, rivers, ocean, winds, heaven. The verbs that link up these nouns together are "mingle" and "mix" which suggest "a law divine" in operation in the universe by which "nothing in the world is single" and one mingles with another's being. In the background of these natural images, the invitation of the poet to his beloved to join him seems quite natural.

In the second stanza, the images that appear are "mountain", "high heaven", "waves", "flower", "sunlight", "the earth", "moonbeams" and "sea" and the verbs that link up the noun are "kiss" and "clasp" explicit gestures of love which did not appear in the first stanza. These images suggest that the entire universe is actively engaged in love. In the background of these images, the poet inspires his beloved to act upon the "divine law of nature" inherent in the images of nature. Then there will be harmony not only in the universe but in the personal world of the poet and his beloved. Rather, they will represent the harmony in the universe.

The structure of the poem is cyclic and repetitive. The verbs of almost the same meaning have been repeated in the poem — "mingle", "mix", "kiss" and "clasp". They multiply the images of harmony. Fountains mingle with the river and the rivers with the ocean. The winds of heaven mix with a sweet emotion. The mountains kiss high heaven. The waves clasp one another. The sunlight clasps the earth. The moonbeams kiss the sea. The entire universe is actively engaged in love. These images demonstrate the law of nature and create a universal atmosphere of harmone. Not only the images but also the rhythm and music of the lines contribute to the atmosphere of harmony. The repetition of soft nasal sounds m, n, the reverberating sound of "r" and sibilant sounds create a harmonious music and the flowing rhythm of the lines contribute to the impression of harmone that pervades the poem.

The poem suggests that reluctance on the part of the beloved would appear unnatural in the background of natural images and would not be in harmony with the rhythm of nature. It is a highly successful poem as its power fully communicates the emotion of the poet through words, images, music and rhythm of the poem.

DARK HOUSE

Dark house, by which once more I stand
Here in the long unlovely street,
Doors, where my heart was used to beat
So quickly waiting for a hand,

A hand that can be clasp'd no more —
Behold me, for I cannot sleep,
And like a guilty thing I creep
At earliest morning to the door.

He is not here; but far away
The noise of life begins again,
And ghastly thro' the drizzling rain
On the bald street breaks the blank day.

—A.L. Tennyson

The poem, "Dark House" is written by Tennyson on the death of his friend, Arthur Henry Hallam. It is part of a longer poem, "In Memoriam". The poem, "Dark House" communicates a sense of deep loss, utter helplessness of the poet and the complete indifference of the mechanical universe to this event.

The first stanza presents the picture of the poet standing by a dark house in the long unlovely street. These are the same unlovely doors where the poet's heart used to beat so quickly waiting for a hand to clasp. But the hand has vanished. The quick heartbeat is absent as the friend is not clasp his hand. The house is no longer a source of light nor the street is lovely to the poet. This is why the house is "dark" and the long street is "unlovely". The poet "cannot sleep" with his grief at the loss of his source of light ("dark") and "beauty" (unlovely) which has made him "creep like a guilty thing". The verb, "creep" is significant. It suggests the life of the poet under the stress of grief.

The absence of the poet's friend has brought about a topsy-turvy in the private and personal world of the poet which is reflected in a series of negative adjectives — "dark" (house), "unlovely" (street), "bald" (street) and "blank" (day) which register the poet's sense of loss of light, loveliness and fulness. The beautiful world of light and loveliness has receded giving way to a strange face of the world. It is not the same world for the poet as the poet's friend "is not here". Yet the world outside the poet has registered no impact of this event. It has remained completely unaffected by this fact and the mechanical processes of the world go on as usual. "The noise of life begins again" and "on the bald street breaks the blank day". The sense of contrast with the world that goes on as usual deepens the desolation of the poet for whom the world has turned bald, blank and unlovely.

THE EDUCATION OF NATURE

Three years she grew in sun and showers
Then Nature said, 'A lovelier flower
On earth was never sown;
This child I to myself will take;
She shall be mine, I will make
A lady of my own.

'Myself to my darling be
Both law and impulse : and with me
The girl, in rock and plain,
In earth and heaven, in glade and bower,
Shall feel an overseeing power
To kindle or restrain.

'She shall be sportive as the fawn
That wild with glee across the lawn

Or up the mountain springs;
And hers shall be the breathing balm,
And her's the silence and the calm
Of mute insensate things.

'The floating clouds their state shall lend
To her; for her the willow bend;
Nor shall she fail to see
E'en in the motions of the storm
Grace that shall mould the maiden's form
By silent sympathy.

'The stars of midnight shall be dear
To her; and she shall lean her ear
In many a secret place
Where rivulets dance their wayward round,
And beauty born of murmuring sound
Shall pass into her face.

'And vital feelings of delight
Shall rear her form to stately height,
Her virgin bosom swell;
Such thoughts to Lucy I will give
While she and I together live
Here in this happy dell.'

Thus Nature spake — The work was done —
How soon my Lucy's race was run!
She died; and left to me
This heath, this calm and quiet scene;
The memory of what has been,
And never more will be.

—W. Wordsworth

William Wordsworth is a poet of nature. He believes that nature's gentle influence moulds the personality into an ideal form. Such is the personality of Lucy in the poem, 'The Education of Nature'. Lucy is the subject of four other poems of Wordsworth. Lucy poems are the unique creations of Wordsworth and this poem is no exception.

The imagery of the first stanza presents Lucy as the loveliest flower-plant growing up in sun and shower. On this ground, the idea of the adoption of Lucy by nature is appropriate. It is the basic metaphor in which the poem is conceived and composed. 'Sun' and 'shower' represent the opposite but necessary forces of nature which mould the personality of Lucy. Thus the personality of Lucy has twin shades which are developed through the poem.

The implications of two symbols, 'sun' and 'shower' are crystallized in the juxtaposition of contraries in the second stanza, law and impulse, kindle and restrain, which are reflected in the contraries inherent in nature, 'rock and plain', 'earth and heaven'. They underline the balanced development of Lucy's personality which is outlined from the third stanza onward. Lucy who lives in a happy dale grows up to acquire a 'stately height'. She grows young ('Her virgin bosom swell'). She is sportive "as the fawn wild with glee across the lawn or the mountain spring" but at the same time she has "silence and calm of mute insensate things". She has at once the majesty of "the floating clouds as well as the humility of willow that bends." She is attracted to the stars of midnight and listens to the music of murmuring river and the beauty of their music passes into her face. Lucy acquires a balanced personality. She is the daughter of nature with the characteristics of fawn, mute, insensate things, clouds, willow, storm and murmuring river. The lines in the last stanza, "The work was done" refers to the above-mentioned developments.

Up to the last stanza there is the objective description of the development of Lucy, the daughter of nature. But for the first time in the last stanza "My" the personal pronoun, "me" precedes "Lucy" which relates her to the poet. This stanza registers a sharp sense of loss at the death of Lucy. Lucy is dead and only "the heath" which is associated with Lucy remains. It is the same scene as usual but with a difference. The adjectives, "calm and quiet" suggest the loss of the presence of Lucy. The scene of the heath is a memento of eternal loss to the poet, "the memory of what has been and never more will be".

GLOSSARY

Alliteration : When two or more than two words in a poetic line begins with the same letter, it is called alliteration.

Assonance : It is the similarity of vowel sounds without the actual rhyme (*e.g.*, "full fathom five thy father lies).

Blank Verse : Blank verse is unrhymed pentameter, not broken into formal units.

Caesura : A pause or break in the line is called caesura.

Hyperbole : Hyperbole is a figure of speech in which exaggeration is used deliberately for the sake of emphasis (*e.g.*, "All the perfumes of Arabia will not sweeten this little hand").

Onomatopoeia : When words echo the sense, it is called onomatopoeia (*e.g.*, "Humming of innumerable bees").

Heroic Couplet : When two iambic pentameters lines rhyme together it is called heroic couplet.

Personification : It is a figure of speech in which lifeless and abstract things are imparted traits of human personality (*e.g.*, "Death lays his icy hands on Kings").

Pun : It consists in a play on the various meanings of a word.

Irony : An ironical statement indicates a meaning contrary to the one it professes to give (*e.g.*, Yet Brutus says he was ambitious,/And Brutus is an honourable man).

Metaphor : It is a figure of speech in which the point of comparison is not stated but implied (*e.g.*, The news you bring is a dagger to my heart).

Simile : A simile is a direct comparison between two different things (*e.g.*, "O my love is like a red, red rose").

Transferred epithet : When the epithet or the qualifying adjective is transferred from the person to the thing, it is called transferred epithet (*e.g.* "The ploughman plods his weary way").

17

Multiple Interpretations : A Practical Guideline

—*Mohit K. Ray*

OURS is an age of criticism, and criticism, in recent years, has become a heavy industry. Gone are the days when it was sincerely believed that a literary work has only one determinate meaning and serious efforts were made to understand what the author means to say. But now, particularly, consequent upon the emergence of post-modernism it is believed that the meaning of a literary work is indeterminate and one hallmark of a good literary work is that it is amenable to multiple interpretations. These ideas had been, in fact, coming in waves from the late nineteenth century, but have been fully crystallized only in recent years. Reacting against earlier schools which focused on the author's biography or the writer's impressions the New Critics concentrated on the poem itself. Since 1960s, however, New Criticism as a theoretical approach has fallen out of favour, because the very idea that the work exists as a self-sufficient object had been challenged. Marxists, feminists and others argue that because a literary work is always bound up with language and social structures, it is never independent and value-free. Now, as we look around, we see that there are a large number of critical theories developed into different schools and their approaches to a literary work are significantly different. Some of the important critical approaches are : Marxist Criticism, New Criticism, Feminist Criticism, Myth Criticism, Archetypal Criticism, Psychoanalytical Criticism, Sexual

Criticism, Linguistic Criticism, Structural Criticism, Deconstruction, Cultural Studies, New Historicism, etc.

It is neither possible nor necessary to discuss these theories; the market is flooded with books on critical theories. However, for the benefit of young learners a short bibliography is provided at the end. What I intent to do here is to suggest guidelines for interpreting a work in the light of different critical theories for the pedagogical purpose of classroom teaching. I have mainly chosen some well-known, frequently anthologized poems so that (i) I don't need to provide the texts of the poems, and (ii) I don't have to develop the point : simple suggestions will do.

Marxist Interpretation

A Marxist interpretation of *The Waste Land* can try to show that *The Waste Land* records the collapse of aristocracy and breakdown of social hierarchies. It can be placed in the background of the Russian Revolution of 1917 and its impact on the political systems of the European countries. Eliot's "a broken Coriolanus" (1.416) can be seen as a symbol of the collapse of aristocracy. Marie, an Austrian aristocrat, articulates the experience of a class in lines 15-18. The lines 191-192 tell us about the death and wreck of kings. In the very opening section the poem is contextualized in Munich, the storm center of contemporary political crisis that reminds us of the overthrow of the Tsarist regime by the Bolshevik Revolution of 1917, the collapse of the Hamburg empire in 1918, the expulsion of Kaisar Wilhelm II of Germany in 1918 etc. The lines 368-378 may be interpreted as describing the rise and spread of communism as a menace to aristocracy where tension and anxiety are reflected in line 138, 'waiting for a knock upon the door'.

It can thus be shown that the poem is eminently amenable to Marxist interpretation.

Similarly a Marxist interpretation of "Kubla Khan" should focus on the enormous wealth of Kubla Khan and the hidden story behind its accumulation, his aristocratic yearning for an earthly paradise, material coverts and sensuous pleasures. He can be seen as an epitome of the exploitation devices as a result of which the general people are not only without a voice but also without any presence in the poem. The Abysinian maid appears only in a vision. A Marxist study of "Sailing to Byzantium" should try to show how Yeast's Irish aristocracy is intended to counteract the middle-class hegemony, and how his Irish nationalism was contradictory to him as he was a bourgeois, Protestant Anglo-Irishman. Even the idea of gold as if permeates his poems in its different associations can be suitably appropriated into a Marxist interpretation.

Feminist Interpretation

A feminist approach to *The Waste Land* would call for a study of the female characters that we meet in the poem, their social positions and Eliot's attitude to and treatment of them. In the first three sections of the poem we meet a number of women characters of different kinds. In the first section we are introduced to Marie, the hyacinth girl, and Madame Sosastris. The second section presents a rich neurotic lady and two women of the lower stratum of the society. The story of Philomel also invokes the picture of a tortured woman. In the third section the seduction of the typist is closely followed by an account of three Thames girls who lost their virginity at different points of the Thames. A close look would reveal that the hyacinth girl — the only girl who is addressed as 'you' — is the ideal woman, a symbol of innocence, beauty and love. All the other women characters contrasted with the hyacinth girl are victims of men's desires. The women we meet in *The Waste Land* are pathetic, wasted women. Their experience is sordid, clandestine and reference to St. Augustine brings home the point that women are agents of sensuality and that they are objects to be rejected or to be pitied. And even Madame Sosastris, "the wisest woman in Europe" cannot make any definite prediction. Eliot's tone is ironical and sarcastic.

A feminist reading of "To His Coy Mistress" would focus on the way the woman is presented in the poem. The focus is on the body of the woman and the speaker in trying to wear down her resistance describes different parts of her body as a series of sexual objects — the eyes, the forehead, the breasts, "the rest" and "every part", and the "marble vault" which is simply a sealed metaphor for the female genital. It may be shown that in the poem the woman is not seen as a complete human being capable of receiving and giving love, but only as an object of sexual pleasure who must be won over through blatant flattery for gratification of the carnal desires.

In order to make a feminist interpretation of a literary work one has to examine how the women are treated, whether they are discriminated against (as in *Tess* or *Anna Karenina*) or they are marginalized or sexually subordinated to man as in Lawrence, or completely ignored as in Tennyson's *Ulysses* or treated as goddesses as in poetry of country love or as temptresses as in Milton's poetry by and large. The main point to see is whether a woman is treated as a complete human being and an equal of man in most respects, or not. And if not, why.

New Criticism

New Criticism focuses on the poem and all other considerations — historical, biographical, sociological, etc. are relegated to the background. The main contention is to see how a work is unified. So a New Critical approach is to examine a poem and try to understand the process of its unification. In the case of *The Waste Land* a close scrutiny would reveal that the poem posits a thematic contrast between two kinds of death and parallels of symbolism of fertility myth and resurrection. The juxtapositional structure reveals diversity in surface similarities and fundamental similarities in apparent dissimilarities and the poem is finally given unity by the unifying consciousness of Tiresias.

A New Critical reading of Yeats's "Sailing to Byzantium" has to first identify the binary oppositions operating in the poem : Becoming/being, sensual/intellectual, here/Byzantium, youth/age, time/eternity etc. and then show how Yeats's use of the word "artifice" in "artifice of eternity" provides the ironic center that unifies the poem.

Similarly, an examination of "Kubla Khan" with the help of New Critical exegesis can show that although the poem has been described as a fragment it is complete in itself. If the first thirty-six lines are concerned with the physical "pleasure dome" in the last eighteen lines there is a transformation of it into a metaphorical pleasure dome represented by the poem itself. The poem finally emerges as "a miracle of rare device" in which polar opposites — fire and ice — are reconciled into a harmonious whole thus illustrating Coleridge's idea of secondary imagination, the esemplastic power. In Shelley's "Ozymandias" the poem is unified by the inscription ("My name is Ozymandias...") on the pedestal of the broken states lying scattered in the desert, that brings the past into a dynamic relationship with the present in which the tyranny of the king is finally superseded by the tyranny of Time.

Myth Criticism

In order to interpret a poem in the light of Myth Criticism it is necessary first to locate the various myths used in a poem and then try to see how these myths contribute to the totality of the poem. In case of *The Waste Land*, for example, one has to examine how the fertility myth, the quest myth (Holy Grail) and the Fisher King myth, among others, account for the substance and the quality of the poem. It is Eliot's imaginative use of the myths that lends support to and reinforces the central theme of the poem.

Archetypal Criticism

Archetypal criticism is close to myth criticism in the sense that both are related to the race memory and the primordial desires of man. But one basic ontological difference is that while an archetype is a figure or a pattern, a myth has always a story element in it. In *The Waste Land* we notice archetypal patterns in the way ideas of the Hanged Man, the chapel perilous, Resurrection etc. are used in the poem. In "Kubla Khan" Kubla emerges as an archetypal figure symbolizing man's eternal yearning for an earthly paradise. Even "the damsel with a dulcimer" can be seen, in the context of the poem, as an archetypal figure representing Muse. Yeats's "Sailing to Byzantium" we can discover a correspondence between Frye's description of the archetypal pattern of comic vision and the poem which has the community of sages, the bird and the city, the geometrical gyre and the archetypal geometrical image of the "starlit dome". In "To His Coy Mistress" in the first stanza we have the picture of an archetypal garden where love can slowly grow into an infinite size. The second stanza destroys the delusion and introduces the desert archetype in terms of naturalistic time. The laws of inevitable decay and death are presented through the archetypal image of Time in a "winged chariot". Furthermore, the archetype of primal fullness is also suggested in lines like "Let us roll our strength and all/Our sweetness into one ball". In Tennyson's "Ulysses" Ulysses emerges as an archetypal figure — a seeker after knowledge, who would like to "follow knowledge, like a sinking star,/ Beyond the utmost bound of human thought". In Shelley's *Prometheus Unbound* as Prometheus chained to the Mount Caucasus approximates the Christ figure and the play, though pagan, becomes increasingly suffused with Christian symbolism, Prometheus becomes an archetypal figure, an embodiment of the spirit of sacrifice for the welfare of the suffering humanity.

Biographical Criticism

The biographical approach is concerned more with the context than with the text. It calls for a detailed study of the historical, biographical circumstances leading to the composition of a poem. It would address itself to the questions like what is the source of the solitary reaper; where and when did Wordsworth meet a "Highland lass" and how does the poem's account of the experience differ from the actual event, etc. In order to make a biographical interpretation of *The Waste Land* one has to go through the biography of Eliot, note the circumstances leading to the composition of the poem and bring to light the autobiographical elements scattered throughout the poem. For the biographical approach to "Kubla Khan" one has to study Coleridge's own statements about the composition of the poem and then compare it with other sources of information — the Crewe Manuscript, for example — to arrive at the truth.

Psychoanalytic Criticism

Psychoanalytic criticism goes one step further. Instead of the external historical details related to the poem the approach is to unmask the poet and try to get hold of the psychological factors operating in the poem. While biographical criticism is concerned with historically verifiable external events psychoanalytic criticism's concern is with the mind of the poet as evidenced in the poem. It is possible then to examine *The Waste Land* in the light of Eliot's experience of the first disastrous marriage, and to see how neurological aberrations of Vivien, Eliot's first wife, and Eliot's own trauma on account of the tumultuous domestic crisis are sublimated into poetry in *The Waste Land*. One can also discern the figure of Emile Hale behind the idyllic portrait of the hyacinth girl. Similarly one can discern the figure of Sarah Hutchinson behind the "damsel with a dulcimer" ("Kubla Khan") once we know about the conjugal disharmony between Coleridge and his wife, Sarah Friekers, and Coleridge's infatuation for Sarah Hutchinson, a beautiful lady with a flair for music.

Sexual Criticism

It is also a form of psychoanalytic criticism but the main concern is to examine how sexuality operates in a poem. The critic tries to interpret the poem in sexual terms. In order to do this it is necessary to examine the images used in a poem very closely and note the sexual overtones and then fit them into a pattern. The slanted deep romantic chasm of "Kubla Khan" for example is overtly sexual. The deep romantic chasm signifies on the surface level a fissure or a gorge on the surface of the earth. In sexual terms it represents the female genital. It is savage because it invites a primordial or instinctive response and it is also holy because it is an instrument of procreation. Shelley's "Ode to the West Wind" has been sexually interpreted as an insistent call by Mary Shelley for a sexual union with her husband after the death of her child Williams, as another poem of Shelley, "The Indian Serenade" has been unmasked as a description of sexual intercourse. In Donne's "The Extasie" in the first line "Where like a pillow on a bed" the simile drops the line into a bedroom and on a bed with a pillow, and once we break the sealed metaphors the first three stanzas can be seen as an elaborate description of the sexual intercourse of the lovers, and this is perfectly in keeping with the importance Donne attaches to the body in the dynamics of body-mind relationship, in the fulfilment of ideal love.

Linguistic Criticism

In order to effect a linguistic interpretation of a poem one has to study the language used and examine how it is related to the theme of the poem. At the simple grammatical level one can show how the abundance of present participles ("breeding", "mixing", "stirring" etc.) which end five of the first seven lines of *The Waste Land* create a sense of movement which is kept up throughout the first eighteen lines. At the level of register one can show how different registers used by different characters in the poem contribute to the polyphonic nature of the poem as transcript of the society. Again at the level of polyglossia — the use of French, German, Italian etc. foregrounds the cosmopolitan, pan-European character of the poem. For linguistic interpretation at the level of registers one has to study who uses a particular register and why and how, and then see how it contributes to the totality of the poem.

Linguistic criticism at the phono-aesthetic level is mainly concerned with the correspondence between the sound and the sense in a poem. One has to examine how the particular collocation of sound reinforces the semantic content of the unit. Take for example, the following lines from Tennyson's "The Lady of Shalott" : "By the margin, willow-veil'd/Slide the heavy barges trail'd/By slow horses and unhail'd/The shallop flitteth silken-sail'd/Skimming down to Camelot". We have two pictures : one of heavy larges trailed by slow horses and the other, a light shallop flitting down to Camelot. It can be shown how the use of clusters of sl (slow, slide) and long vowels (barges, margin, trailed etc.) makes reading to the first two and half lines quite difficult. We experience the heaviness of the barges full of commercial commodities in reading the lines. In fact the barges are so heavy that the horses have to stop in the middle of the line to take breath as it were.... But by contrast the liquid 'i's (shallop, flitteth, silken-sail'd) and the short vowels (flitteth, silken, skimming) contribute to the lightness and speed of the shallop. Similarly, the conflicting feelings of expansiveness and constriction of the modern man can be perfectly conveyed by open, expansive sound pattern ("The evening is spread out against the *sky*") and use of closely punctuated words with locking consonants ("like a patient, etherized upon a table").

Structural Criticism

Structuralist approach to a poem which originally consisted in the application of the insights of structural linguistics to a literary work has now widened to take into consideration, in addition to the linguistic structure of a poem, other structures such as the ideational structure, the imagistic structure, the signic structure and the symbolic structure etc. It stems from the belief that the text is a kind of formless space whose shape is imposed by structuralist modes of reading. The concepts derived from structural linguistics, if intelligently applied to a literary work, can explain its structure and meaning. It can then provide a kind of discovery procedure which has been effectively used by Roman Jakobson and Anthony L. Johnson. At the physical level we have the structural units in the stanzas or parts of a poem, and one can examine how these structural units are unified by the ideational content of the poem and its development from a beginning through a middle to an end. But what is more important is to see how the poem is structured by certain recurring images (imagistic structure), certain ideas and binary oppositions (ideational structure), certain arrangement of signs (semiotic structure) and the symbols scattered throughout the poem (symbolist structure) etc. In "Sailing to Byzantium" the imagistic and signic structures run counter to the ideational structure which is composed of binary oppositions (time/eternity, youth/age, art/self, body/soul, etc.). The binary oppositions are subverted by the semantically complex bird images as well as the signic "I" which condenses many contradictory meanings. Finally, it can be seen that the poet provides the model of the transforming creative act by fusing the poetic "I" with the bird-song to constitute "the artifice of eternity". Structural criticism has some affinity with New Criticism in its close reading of the text and in its interest in the discovery of the binary oppositions in the ideational matrix of the poem, but it goes beyond New Criticism and looks forward to Semiotics or the study of signs and Genre Criticism.

Genre Criticism

A generic approach to a poem has to first consider the genre or the literary form (novel, poetry, drama etc.) or the subgenre (autobiographical novel, pastoral poetry, tragedy etc.) in which it is formally placed, and then examine its structure and the texture closely to see whether it actually belongs to the genre or the subgenre in which it is placed. *The Rape of the Lock*, for example, has been described as a "heroi-comical poem" but a close scrutiny of its five cantos and its texture clearly reveals that it is a dramatic poem. Its five cantos perfectly correspond to the five acts of a drama. Similarly, the passion-oriented texture of a novel like *Wuthering Heights* and its lyrical flow of the language would suggest that it is more a dramatic poem than a novel. What is the exact genre of *The Waste Land*? It begins in the form of narrative ("April is the cruelest month...") but with the introduction of the first person plural in the eighth line ("Summer surprised us") it assumes the form of a monologue and we presume that it is a monologue of Marie ("He said, Marie, Marie hold on tight"). But as we proceed we realize that personae change and one character melts into another. So, it cannot be called a monologue. Can we call it s drama because the poem is divided into five parts? But, again, a close scrutiny reveals that there is no dramatic development. Nor can we call it an anti-drama, because if it does not conform to the dramatic convention it does not revolt against it either. In view of its elegiac tone we can try to define it as an elegy, but that also is not possible because it does not conform to any standard forms of elegy; moreover the hectic disordered vision of the concluding lines is inimical to the elegiac catharsis where the poem ends on a note of reintegration at a higher level. Thus a generic interpretation would show that the poet defies any standard label; what we have is not a particular genre but a generic constellation, a cluster of genres created by multiple voices, multiple points of view and inter-textuality.

Deconstructive Criticism

The question that often baffles our young teachers is : how to deconstruct a literary work? What are the possible strategies? What should be the procedure? The best way to deconstructive criticism is to start on the New critical line, identify the mechanics of coherence and unity in the light of New Criticism and then turn round and point out the gaps in the argument, the lacunae, the elements of wishful thinking and thus turn the text against itself. Take, for example, *The Waste Land*. In his "Notes on *The Waste Land*" Eliot says : "What Tiresias *sees*, in fact, is the substance of the poem". But, in the first place, Tiresias is blind; then how can he see? If Eliot means that the real sight is insight — his emphasis on the word "sees would imply that — even then Tiresias is not the only prophet in the poem. There are, to begin with, the Cumean Sibyl whose placement in the epigraph suggests that she subsumes all figures including Tiresias. In other words if what Tiresias sees is the substance of the poem what's wrong with, the Cumean Sybil or a minor seer like Madame Sosastris? There are so many seers and Eliot oversees them all. Then about the substance of the poem. The ontological nature of a poem implies that the substance of a poem is the poem itself. Then how can we make a substance of the poem? We are equally unsure about the functions of the symbols. Fire is a frequently used symbol in *The Waste Land*. But what does it symbolize? Lust or purification? Is it pentecostal fire or purgatorial fire? when a word is made to symbolize diverse things it fails to act as a symbol. For a change, now let us look at "Sailing to Byzantium". A deconstructive reading will follow the text's oppositions and notice how the text appears to resolve its oppositions; but it must go further to show how the resolution, a wishful thinking, falls apart. We have only to focus on the utterance in the final stanza, "Once out of nature I shall never take/My bodily from any natural thing" and point out that it amounts to asking for the moon, asking for an impossibility, the simple fact being that whatever bodily form one takes — the form of a bird or simply the golden form embodied by an artist it must be taken from nature. In other words, art is already present in nature. Whether we think of a golden apple or a centaur or a chimera they can be shown to be an assemblage of different objects of nature; every part can be traced back to nature. As nobody can cross his own shadow similarly nobody can go out of nature even in his imagination. The kind of indeterminacy that we noticed in Eliot's use of symbols can also be detected in this poem. When, for example, the soul is made to "sing, and louder/For every tatter in its mortal dress" how do we know whether the soul is singing in spite of physical ailments or to distract itself from the tatters of the mortal dress, or it is singing in celebration of these tatters because it brings the soul closer to its liberation from the body? How to deconstruct a poem like "Ulysses"? Now traditionally the poem presents Ulysses as a great savant, and untiring seeker after knowledge. To him experience is knowledge, and the loudly proclaims : "...all experience is an arch wherethro'/Gleams that untravell'd world, whose margin fades/For ever and for ever when I move". If all experience is an arch why can't Ulysses derive knowledge from his present experience at Ithaca? Studied more closely it will be evident that he is actually an egoist and an escapist. He wants to abdicate his responsibility as a king and as a father and go abroad not really in search of knowledge but in search of self-glorification. The hypocrisy of the man becomes clearer when we notice that the concluding line of the poem ("to strive, to seek, to find, not to yield") is an echo of Satan's resolution in *Paradise Lost*.

SELECT BIBLIOGRAPHY

Bennet, Andrew and Nicolas Royle, *An Introduction to Literature, Criticism and Theory*. Hertfordshire : Prentice Hall, 1995.

Bressker, Charles F., *Literary Criticism : An Introduction to Theory and Practice*. New Jersey : Prentice Hall, 1994.

Buchbinder, David, *Contemporary Literary Theory and the Reading of Poetry*. Melbourne, Macmillan Education Australia Pvt. Ltd., 1993.

Guerin, Wilfred L., Earle Labor *et al.* eds., *A Handbook of Critical Approaches to Literature*. Oxford : Oxford University Press, 1999.

Lodge, David, ed., *20th Century Literary Criticism : A Reader*. London : Longman, 1972.

Lynn, Steven, *Texts and Contexts : Writing About Literature and Critical Theory*. New York : Harper Collins, 1994.

Moody, H.L.B., *Literary Appreciation : A Practical Guide*. London : Longman, 1987.

Ryan, Michael, *Literary Theory : A Practical Introduction*. Oxford : Blackwell, 1999.

Selden, Raman, *A Reader's Guide to Contemporary Literary Theory*, Kentucky : Kentucky University Press, 1989.

Staton, Shirley F., ed., *Literary Theories in Praxis*. Philadelphia : Philadelphia University Press, 1987.

18

Filling an Empty Container : A Practical Exercise

—Rama Kundu

"A text is an empty container waiting to be filled with meanings."

—Frank Lentricchia on Stanley Fish (147)

Professor Mohit K. Ray in his illuminating and scholarly study of "The Genealogy of Postmodernism" uses the metaphor of the "Serbonian bog" to indicate the baffling richness of critical response *vis-a-vis* the phenomenon known as postmodernism.

> "To come to postmodernism is to enter the great Serbonian bog where whole armies have sunk" (Ray 2001 : 24).

Postmodernism is, indeed, a concept/term/practice that baffles any attempt at definition, and expectedly so, since its chief characteristics are multiplicity and provisionality. Even Linda Hutcheon, in her voluminous and scholarly book *A Poetics of Postmodernism* but evidences this honest bafflement at the insufferably variegated, though delightful, intellectual-cultural fiesta of postmodernism. As Professor Ray succinctly underpins in his essay, postmodernism is characterized by the energy which is derived from the rethinking of the value of multiplicity and provisionality in actual practice — both creative and critical; and in the process basically it challenges the very notion of coherence.

In the field of literary criticism the result has been almost unhinging so far as traditional notions of 'order'/'center' are concerned. Not only does it prevent glossing over contradictions; the critic's desire to find a "center" comes to be considered a kind of wish-fulfilment, and any such attempt at "center"-ing comes to be dismissed as "the useless legacy of the old metaphysics" (Ray : 26). De-centering, as Ray explains, implied the assumption that outside discourse there is no fixed point from which one can establish metaphysical boundaries for legitimate signifiers.

In such a situation criticism becomes simultaneously a creative activity as well, and the reader/critic eventually acquires the status of co-author. As result, the text, or rather the subtext[s] emerge/s out of the vital interconnection between the text and the reader. One may recall Stanley Fish's notion which has become almost a cliché — that a text is an empty container waiting to be filled with meanings. This assumption that positive knowledge is not available, that there can be no determinacy or objective reading, — along with the isolation of the text, its divorce from the signifier, its reliance on the signified — all these have led to a kind of intellectual anarchy. With the stability of a work being challenged an anarchy of interpretation has taken place. It seems that there is no reading but misreading, and no text but only subtexts. Denial of authority has apparently led critics to fantasize, to write fiction instead of criticism to spin webs of personal and/or private associations.

Robert Kroetsch, the renowned post-modern writer-critic of Canada today, has underscored this creative role of the reader-critic-co-author in the context of postmodernism. In an interview of 1976 he said : "I think that critical task is really an exciting one, of finding ways to talk about this new work and to assess it, because the critic is still a mediator between the poet and the audience, and there is no use pretending that he isn't." But, at the same time, Kroetsch also took care to point out : "Being a mediator…is a demanding task right now. You are not just filling in the blanks, you are making maps". This is but voicing a common postmodern notion, though a bit metaphorically, that a text is now to the critic an uncharted world open to infinite variety of forms and ways of explorations and investigations and admitting the necessary uncertainties or tenativeness involved in the process of such cartography. [One may also recall the complex and shifting foci which the terms cartography, psychocartography in especial have assumed in the postcolonial era.[1]] Stanley Fish's famous lecture of 1980, "Is There a Text in this Class?" had its share in popularizing this trend — already on the surge — of multiple interpretations by emphasizing the instability of the text and unavailability of determinate meanings, although Fish himself would have perhaps preferred limited indeterminacy and a situational definition of meanings.

It is against this backdrop that I shall like to share an experience of mine with the reader. Some months ago I had this delightful experience of practical criticism following the 'Fish'-y way. The occasion was a routine Group Discussion by the participants in a UGC-sponsored Refresher Course in English for college and university teachers, held by the Academic Staff College, Burdwan University. The well-known four-line nursery rhyme — 'Humpty Dumpty sat on a wall…' etc. was used as the hypothetical "empty container waiting to be filled with meanings", and the participants, one by one, did their share in the job of "filling". The result was simply fantastic in its variety, playfulness, penetration, incoherence, indeterminacy, anarchy of interpretations.

Here I have summed up the entire discussion with minimum editing so that the reader can get a whiff of the mood — playful and adventurous — that flavoured the hours-long exercise in interpreting the four lines. P. will mean participant; real names are withheld for obvious reasons. Intelligent, tricky, and illuminating questions were raised in response to almost all the speakers, which I have not been able to incorporate in details. These questions were generally addressed by the speakers, — with patience, ambience, readiness to accommodate, an openness which is the hallmark of postmodern criticism.

P.1. maintains that the text, though 'supposed' to be but a nursery rhyme, may still be considered in the light of archetypal criticism; it reworks an archetypal theme, *i.e.*, fall of man. The "wall" thus comes to epitomise the walled garden of Paradise. Humpty, Dumpty are re-playing the story of man's first disobedience; their very act of climbing up the wall may suggest a posture of inordinate wilfulness, and naturally "fall" — which is also "great" — must be the inevitable conseqence. "King" is, of course, God, and "king's men" are angels; but what about the "horses"?

P.2. considers it an allegory, but it is an unusual allegory in the sense that here good and evil, *i.e.* Humpty and Dumpty are fighting, but both fall as result of the fighting, and are destroyed. So he is not sure about the moral message that is to be derived from this grim allegory where everything seems to get lost in total anarchy. Again, he admits, the neat pattern of parallels that are to be expected in an allegory also seems to be missing.

P.3. examines the lines in the light of Marxist criticism. He explains it as man's fall from the idyllic happiness of primitive communism; since the "great fall" the feudal lord has accumulated cattle "horses" and slaves ("men"), but has failed to restore man to primitive happiness.

When the listeners pointed out the sequential issue, — whether it is factually valid to hold that the two historical processes followed one another in such quick succession, and also wanted to know how to explain the "wall" or the nomenclature of the subject[s] in line 1, P.3./became angry and sullen. Limitations of orthodoxy! But postmodernism is prepared to make fun of all "closed", "ultimate", "absolutist" conclusions. So there.

P.4. prefers to read it as a paradigmatic love story of the catastrophic kind. Humpty is the Prince or rich man's son or minister's son; Dumpty is the poor girl with no connections, or *vice-versa*. Because of social and familial hostilities which prove too much to overcome the lovers strike a suicide pact. "Fall" is death, — falling dead. The "king" is the patriarch figure — figurehead of the patriarchal — hierarchical society. Once the tragedy takes place no effort, however pompous, of the patriarchal society can undo it.

P.5. reads into it a romantic love story about happy love. Humpty and Dumpty were lovers. They "fell" in love; then, eventually they "fell" in each other's arms and their love was consummated. After this gets known authoritarian attempts are made at social or familial levels to sunder them. But the lovers successfully thwart all such attempts. She dwells on the word "together" from an interesting angle, only two *different* things, she argues, can be put "together". But when they have already merged into 'one', any attempt at putting them together becomes redundant, preposterous and comical.

P.6. brings the feminist angle. Humpty is a man, Dumpty a woman. Here we have the prefiguring, foregrounding of the male, *i.e.* Humpty. It is but symptomatic of the patriarchal culture that the female is made to play the follower role; her ups and downs are but inseparably tied up with the male master's fate, his climbing (on the wall or social success) and his crash. Humpty is thus the assertive male-master-husband; Dumpty the meek female-subservient-wife.

P.7. thinks that both Humpty and Dumpty are men; it is an exclusive situation; for men only. And Humpty-Dumpty, sitting (*i.e.* living) on the wall, that is the exclusive no-woman area, get bored, then angry; knowing not what to do the two angry men start fighting, and fall. According to P.7, it is only women who have the ability of crisis-management. But since there is no woman here, and everything is left in the hand of male power and militancy, —"king", "men", and "horses" signifying this male [mis]management — it is but natural that the situation should get out of hand.

P.8. guesses about the possibility of a male writer behind the text. P.8. notes a preponderance of the male world; there is no name or surname, nor any pronoun to overtly suggest a female figure. Women have been silenced and absenced from this text. Normally boys are supposed to climb up a stiff wall, not girls. This is a text about a masculine world of physical activity, glamorous show of pomp and power which might interest boys, but which completely ignored and excluded girls. An instance of covert but strong chauvinism!

P.9. interprets the text from the postcolonial perspective. Seen thus Humpty stand for the imperial power of Europe; Dumpty is the ethnic identity of the far away colony, say Australia. From the very beginning it was an uneasy relationship. "Wall" suggests the precariousness of the situation; "fall", therefore was but an inevitable consequence — say a historical necessity. Eventually it happens, though when it happens at last it looks "great", irredeemable as it is. "King" is king of England or the European imperial power. "Horses" and "men" are the militarial and political devices of the West to maintain political *status quo* in the colonies. In the eventuaity of a real show down these do not come to any real help.

P.10. This could be a postcolonial parody of colonial assumptions. Both Humpty and Dumpty are flagbearers of the hegemonic power. The names conjure a picture of opulence, — a pair of well-fed, complacent, generals they may be. At the beginning they are shown sitting complacently in their bastion of imperial power, they do not know when things have fallen apart. Their downfall which takes them unaware is both disastrous and comic as well as irretrievable like the course of history.

P.11. It is carnivalesque fun at the highly placed officials or royal people, at their show of pomp and pride, and their comical discomfiture on occasions. P.11. shows how the parodic effect is secured by means of semantic and sonic suggestions. If read aloud the 1st and the 3rd lines re-enact the sound of hollow drum-beats, self-advertising noise, the ridiculous humbug of imperial pomp and pride. The 2nd and the 4th lines bring out the fun of the fall which is beyond repair, although disproportionately fastidious or fussy attempts are made to do the repairing. "Great" may have been used ironically in the context.

P.12. offers a historicist interpretation and reads it as the story of the distintegration of the Empire. Humpty and Dumpty, sitting together, may be regarded as icons of British imperialism.

Sitting smugly on the "wall" implies the sanctimonious stand of superiority. It is the posture of holding aloof — arrogantly and snobbishly. The fall and the subsequent exercises in futility are part of the post-war history of the world.

P.14. assures us that here is a sealed metaphor for sexual consummation. Humpty and Dumpty are the male and female. The "wall" is the manifold inhibitions — social-moral-cultural-psychological etc. The lovers overcome this and fall for each other. Once the sex act takes place chastity/virginity/celibacy is lost; the hymen is broken.

P.15. looks at the text from the angle of sociolgoical criticism and claims that Humpty Dumpty are representatives of the common, poor, humdrum people. "Wall" suggests their marginalization. They are pushed to the verge and destroyed whereas the forces at power only pretend to act, and that too after they have been already ruined.

P.16. The humble and the dumb of the society are all the time on the borderline between survival and collapse. Yet there comes a time when the establishment has to acknowledge the enormity of the collapse. But then it is beyond their power of recovery.

P.17. Humpty and Dumpty represent a series of binaries of the society. Humpty is the humbug/egoistic/husband/leader/exploiter; Dumpty is the dumb/to-be-dumped/wife/humble follower/victim/exploited. "Wall" suggests the precariousness of the situation, that sooner or later there will be confrontation. When this ultimately happens no authoritarian force can prevent the ensuing chaos.

P.18. Humpty and Dumpty represent the people of two different communities. The "sitting" together at the beginning refers to their congenial relationship at a time of stability and peace. But the peace is destroyed by sudden dislocation which may have been caused by communal or ethnic violence. As result stability and harmony of the society are shattered and there follow crisis, trauma, war and chaos.

P.19. It is a case of schizophrenia leading to the disintegration of the self; in such a psychological situation not external factor or outsider can restore the integral self.

P.20. It is an existential crisis faced by the individual who does not find his identity in the big chaotic world ruled by the Absurd. The crisis is the result of the individual's alienation from the walled security of family or society.

P.21. looks at the text form the angle of genre criticism. It could be considered a tragedy. In the story of the Bible there is the explicitly stated hope that ultimately man should be restored to bliss; but here the fall remains the final catastrophic event with no hope of redemption in near or distant future.

P.21 also conjectures about the author: who is the author? What may be his social-political-marital situation that he should be so pessimistic? Is it possible that a personal tragedy of the author operates behind such bleak imaginings?

P.22. finds it a comedy with the typical comic sequences, and comic exaggerations as signified by "great", "all". It is basically the laughter of farce that has been generated here. P.22 also mentions in this connection the typical illustrations of the rhyme in children's books in which Humpty and Dumpty are portrayed as clown figures with large hats, pot-bellied bodies, and funny air of self-importance.

P.23. If it's a question of genre then of course it is closer to the ballad than any other category of narration. Like a ballad it is purely action-oriented. Events quickly follow one another as in a ballad. The indifference to character-study or to the motive is also in tune with the ballad narration. So are the economy and impersonality of the narratorial mode.

P.24. studies from a historian's point of view. Recalls Gibbon's *The Decline and Fall*... P.24 also reads into the four lines three strands of history : (i) the history of the fall of monarchy; (ii) the history of the disintegration of a country thanks to the insincere efforts of its ruler who tries to solve crucial and delicate problems of healing a scarred nation only by activating the war machinery — "men" and "horses" suggesting infantry and cavalry respectively. That they should fail is but a foregone conclusion; (iii) the history of the fall of the autocrat who sits on the high wall, that is, makes himself inaccessible. He sits tight, comfortable, complacent for some time. But the fall must come sooner or later; when it comes in the end it is a great fall.

P.25. studies it from the position of new historicism. According to P. 25 the text underscores the centrality of little persons; though humble (Humpty) and dumb (Dumpty), still they may aspire to reach high (wall); and even when they fail they can create great commotions which may not be ignored by the big people in the social hierarchy.

P.26. It is the crisis of the modern society. It has lost the stability and security it was supposed to possess in the past. The stability and security in the past, which was itself ironically precarious as indicated by "wall" — a wall is not a safe place for relaxing — is now gone for ever. Neither animal instinct (horses), nor human intellect (men) can restore it.

P.27. considers the text from the perspective of culture study. A rhyme may have hidden meanings as it comes up from folk-memory. An interpretation of a rhyme should be, therefore, related to culture studies. Seen thus the present rhyme appears to have been a record of some great accident/collective trauma/ some memorable tragedy involving children of high families which had probably entered the domain of folk-memory. P.27 also admits that this may be the story of a failed marriage which is so common everywhere, and also conjectures if in future the story of the famous failed marriage — of Prince Charles and Diana — may get strung to this text as a footnote.

Or could it be the memory of some great devastating earthquake?

P.28. examines it from the point of view of narratology. He says it is a sort of metafiction, — a story about the dislocation of narrative forms in fiction. In traditional story-telling story and plot (Humpty and Dumpty) went happily together, and enjoyed a kind of stable, secure relationship. In postmodern times the symmetrical coherence of traditional fiction has broken down. The binaries also bear out this meaning : wall=symmetry; fall=disjunction; horses-books; men-readers.

P.29. also makes a narratological approach, but from another angle. She maintains that we can take it as a description of the process by which subversion of a canonical text takes place in the postcolonial practice. Humpty and Dumpty are thus meant to signify respected canonical texts which had enjoyed the status of cultural superiority till the postcolonial writers of the third world began to subvert them. After that no political or ideological effort can help them regain their earlier status.

P.30. examines the text after the New Critical fashion. She dwells on the ambiguities. We are just told that Humpty Dumpty "sat". But we are not told if they were sitting together or separately. What was the posture? Was it a lovers' embrace or friends' intimacy? Were they sitting casually side by side, or angrily apart, sullenly or sadly, absent mindedly or indifferently? These questions remain unanswered. Then how did they fall? If they had been sitting quietly then there would have been no occasion for falling. Were they restive or quarrelling? If so, why? If they had not been "together" earlier (being torn apart by mutual hostility) then the business of putting them together by external agencies was bound to be frustrating. Or was the wall an old tottering structure, cracked and crumbling which came down suddenly and thus caused the disaster? Or did it come down because of an earthquake?

Again, who is or are Humpty Dumpty? Are they two people, or is it one name and a surname denoting a single person? What is the sex of the person/s? There is no reference to the sex of Humpty Dumpty.

Again, which side of the wall did they fall? Inside or outside? A lot depends on which way we interpret it. If they fall outside that should mean a positive message, — an escape from some walled city/prison. If they fall inside that means a negative message, — permanent imprisonment/life-term,/the prospect of an endless nightmare 'in the penal colony'. By the by, is it likely that Humpty Dumpty are but two daring jail-breakers.

P.31. holds that this could be studied in the light of a postmodern parody of all serious, heroic, and tragic stories of "great fall"s to be found in the metanarratives of literature, culture and history. Even the sound pattern is made to contribute to the parodic effect. The sonic effect of the first two lines suggests a gaudy procession; that of the last two lines suggests chaos.

P.32. Insists that the text belongs to the domain of nonsense literature and we, therefore, should not look for any meaning into it. Any attempt to locate a meaning or 'text' is bound to ruin the enjoyment of the rhyme, and is also bound to be necessarily far-fetched. However, even the claim of uninterpretability is a kind of interpretation!

If there had been more participants we would surely have even more of such 'interpretations'. But even as it is, here we had a wide array of interpretations, extremely varied and often quite interesting as they were, which had been brought to bear on the text. Every meaning could be illuminating in a way, not only about the text but perhaps more so about the critic's attitude and disposition. Still no single analysis was final; a chink or chinks remained through which other meanings crowded in. The exercise shows that criticism could also be a game and fun, though a game made special and colourful by the play of imagination, and surprising insights, where the reader/critic continued to usurp/share the author's godly province and put into practice what Terence Hawkes claimed in the conclusion to his essay on Shakespeare — "We *make* texts mean". At the end of his excellent summing up of the new critical approaches to Shakespeare Terence Hawkes observes :

> "A major and developing area of recent critical activity...involves the study of the degree to which all texts are always read from particular points of view all the time.

> The 'essential' text, it seems to follow is never genuinely available to us....[It has been] a general shift of interest from the author of the text to its reader....
>
> The first principle of such studies must be that no text means by itself : no text has a single, essential untransformable meaning to which, when all criticism is said and done, we can finally turn. We *make* texts mean, the argument runs, and the positions from which we do so constitute a major aspect of the meanings we produce."

The authorship and date of composition of the present rhyme are not known, though there is evidence that in the nineteenth century England it was already a well-known popular nursery rhyme as Lewis Carroll's little Alice had personally met Humpty Dumpty in course of her dream-journey 'through the looking glass' and had a long discussion with him on various matters including the rhyme about him. Before concluding we may have a look at the encounter between Carroll's Alice (in *Through the Looking Glass*) and Humpty Dumpty which took place more than a century ago. One is struck by the way Carroll's Humpty Dumpty, one person, jumps out of the nursery textbook to enjoy an extratextual status of his own in Carroll's text, and makes exemplary discourse — so very much ahead of his time too — on the particular subject of 'making' 'meanings' of 'words' and 'poems'.

In Chapter Five of *Through the Looking Glass* Alice goes to buy an egg from a sheep; it is here that she finds one egg getting larger and larger, and "more and more human", and coming closer she "saw clearly that it was HUMPTY DUMPTY himself" (208). In the subsequent chapter there is a long dialogue between the egg-man and Alice. As expected he sits on the top of a high wall, with his legs crossed like a Turk. Alice is apprehensive that he may slip but he proudly assures her about the King's promise :

> Here he pursed up his lips, and looked so solemn and grand that Alice could hardly help laughing. "*If* I did fall," he went on, "*the King has promised me* — ah, you may turn pale, if you like! You didn't think I was going

> to say that, did you? *The King has promised me — with his very own mouth* — to — to —"

"To send all his horses and all his men" Alice interrupted; rather unwisely.

Humpty Dumpty is extremely annoyed at this :

> "Now I declare that's too bad!" Humpty Dumpty cried, breaking into a sudden passion. "You've been listening at doors — and behind trees — and down chimneys — or you couldn't have known it!"

Alice pleads gently :

> "I haven't indeed!... It's in a book."

At the mention of 'Book' Humpty Dumpty is appeased :

> "Ah, well! They may write such things in a *book*", Humpty Dumpty said in a calmer tone. "That's what you call a History of England, that is."

And the egg-man makes claim to his special position in the 'History of England" as "one that has spoken to a King". In kind condescension to Alice he says : "mayhap you'll never see such another : and to show you I'm not proud, you may shake hands with me!" And he grins from ear to ear has he leans forwards (almost to the point of falling from the wall in doing so) and offers Alice his hand (210).

In course of their long discussion on poetry and various other items Alice for once contests his whimsical use of words with wrong meanings, — 'glory', for example.

"I don't know what you mean by 'glory'", Alice said.

Humpty Dumpty smiled contemptuously. "Of course you don't — till I tell you. I meant 'there's a nice knockdown argument for you!' "

Alice objects, "But 'glory' doesn't mean a 'nice knock-down arugment'."

H.D. assures her :

"When I use a word, ... it means just what I choose it to mean — neither more nor less."

"The question is", said Alice, "whether you *can* make words mean so many different things."

"The question is," said Humpty Dumpty, "which is to be master — that's all" (214).

When Alice complains, "That's a great deal to make one word mean", H.D. again assures her :

> "When I make a word do a lot of work like that, I always pay it extra" (214).

This Humpty Dumpty also evinces perfect confidence regarding his own ability of critical interpretation :

> "I can explain all the poems that ever were invented — and a good many that haven't been invented just yet" (215). Could it be cited as a devastating critique of professional criticism itself!

Anyway, there is a word in Humpty Dumpty's lexicon which may be welcome to the reader right now; it is "impenetrability". Humpty Dumpty explains to the child with obvious pleasure : "I meant by 'impenetrability' that we've had enough of that subject..." (214).

NOTE

1. Nayantara Sehgal in her essay "The Myth Re-Incarnated" in *Journal of Commonwealth Literature*, Vol. xxx, No. 1, 1995 explains how a changing map of the world affects the concept of identity. She holds that what one perceived as civilization, and what as outer darkness depended on one's location : "The 300-odd years of Europe's maritime age — exploration, conquest, colonization and empire — created a lasting psycho-cartography, positioning Europe and the Atlantic as fount and centre, and all the rest as outlying and peripheral, created for serving and servicing the centre. Areas were labelled Near, Middle of Far, depending on their distance from the centre and were judged by their usefulness to it. The reigning reality divided the map into rulers and the lesser breed they ruled, a master race and subject races.

WORKS CITED

Carroll, L., *The Complete Works*, N.Y. The Modern Library (n.d.).

Fish, Stanley, *Is There a Text in this Class? The Authority of Interpretive Communities*. Combridge Harvard University Press, 1980.

Hawkes, T., "Shakespeare and New Critical Approaches", in *The Cambridge Companion to Shakespeare Studies* [Ed. Stanley Wells]. Cambridge : Cambridge University Press, 1986.

Hutcheon, Linda. *A Poetics of Postmodernism*. N.Y.; London : Routledge, 1988.

Kroetsch, R., "Uncovering Our Dream World : An Interview with Robert Kroetsch" in *Arts Manitoba* (a bi-monthly magazine of arts) V. 1, No. 1, Jan-Feb., 1977.

Lenricchia, Frank, *After the New Criticism*. London : Methuen, 1980.

Ray, Mohit K., *Studies in Literary Criticism*. New Delhi : Atlantic Publishers and Distributors, 2001.

LIST OF CONTRIBUTORS

A.K. Awasthi, Professor, Department of English, Dr. H.S. Gaur University, Sagar, Madhya Pradesh.

Asit Biswas, Reader in English, Bankura Christian College, Bankura, West Bengal.

Sukriti Ghosal, Reader in English, B.K. Girls' College, Howrah, West Bengal.

K.M. Jan, Department of English, M.S. College, Motihari, Bihar.

Anjani Kumar, Department of English, G.D. College, Begusarai, Bihar.

Bimalendu Kundu, Senior Lecturer in English, Durgapur Women's College, Durgapur, West Bengal.

Rama Kundu, Professor of English, Burdwan University, Burdwan, West Bengal.

Samiran Majilya, Lecturer in English, M.U.C. Women's College, Burdwan, West Bengal.

Mallikarjun Patil, Lecturer, Department of English, Gulbarga University, Gulbarga, Karnataka.

Mohit K. Ray, Professor of English, Burdwan University, Burdwan, West Bengal.

Sushma Sharma, Head and Reader, K.G.K. Postgraduate College, Moradabad, Uttar Pradesh.

Krishna Singh, Assistant Professor, Department of English, Govt. P.G. College, Shahdol, Madhya Pradesh.

S.P. Singha, Reader in English, Vidyasagar University, Midnapore, West Bengal.

M.P. Sinha, Professor and Head, Department of English, Kanpur University, Kanpur.

V. Sujatha, Rashtriya Sanskrit Vidyapeeth Tirupati, Andhra Pradesh.